A PRACTICAL GUIDE FOR

Student Writers

RICHARD LEVESQUE, PH.D.

Boston Burr Ridge, IL Dubuque, IA New York San Francisco St. Louis
Bangkok · Bogotá Caracas Lisbon London Madrid
Mexico City Milan New Delhi Seoul Singapore Sydney · Taipei Toronto

The McGraw-Hill Companies

A Practical Guide for Student Writers

12 13 14 15 QVR QVR 13

ISBN-13: 978-0-07-803984-3
ISBN-10: 0-07-803984-3

Learning Solutions Specialist: Kelly Casey
Production Editor: Jennifer Pickel
Cover Design: Felicia Cornish
Printer/Binder: Quad/Graphics

TABLE OF CONTENTS

Introduction: What Are We Doing Here?

As students in a Developmental Writing course, you probably have some expectations and some questions about just what this course will do for you and why you have been placed in it. The first thing you should be aware of is that this class is designed to prepare you for the next course in the sequence, usually labeled "Freshman Composition" or something similar. In that class, you will be expected to write in a very specific way, known as Academic Discourse.

Academic Discourse can loosely be explained as the "language of the academy." In other words, it's the set of rules to which most college-level writing is expected to conform. This can include things like word choice, paper format, levels of formality, and grammar, to name a few. It also has to do with sophistication of ideas.

As a writer, you may already be strong in some of these areas, but in others you need to improve, and that is what this Developmental Writing course is primarily designed to help you with.

Becoming a Better Writer

You may have some preconceptions about what it means to write well. Some of these may be accurate and others not so much. Regardless, one thing you should be aware of is that writing well is difficult for everyone. There are some people who make it look easy and others who seem to be able to produce beautiful work in one draft, but usually even those writers are constantly crafting their work in their heads before writing a word.

To move yourself in the right (or is "write"?) direction, here are a few principles to consider:

- Writers write
- Good writers read
- Good writing is rewriting

Writers Write. This may seem like a no-brainer, but you can't become a better writer by just talking about it. You actually have to do it. A student in this class should get used to writing *something* every day: journal entries, drafts, responses to reading, etc. It all counts. The more you get used to putting words on paper and thinking about the best combinations of words and phrases, the stronger you will become as a writer.

Good Writers Read. Perhaps this should be amended to "Good Writers Read Good Writing." One way to improve your writing is to drill yourself with grammar and writing exercises, but another way is to read as much as you can. This second method is usually more fun and more productive. If you read carefully and consciously, paying attention not only to what other writers say but to *how* they say it, you will begin to develop an ear for what sounds right, for what appeals to you as a reader, and for what does not. The more you do this, the sooner you will find that you begin to imitate and emulate the writing you find compelling and interesting.

Good Writing Is Rewriting. As noted earlier, even the best writers struggle, and perhaps the best of the best struggle the most with the words on the page. Welsh poet Dylan Thomas was noted for listing lengthy columns of words as he crafted his poems, searching for just the right one. To read the finished product, though, one would never know how hard he worked. Again, the best writers make it *look* easy. You shouldn't be worried about that. Instead, you should focus on producing the best material you can. This involves using the Writing Process (to be covered later), allowing yourself to draft material that is rough the first time around and then giving yourself the time to polish and revise, making the work stronger each time you go over it.

This Sounds Like a Lot of Work

Writing well does, in fact, involve a lot of work, and as a college student, you need to be aware that work is connected to time. The amount of time you put into this class will directly affect your success in it. If you do the bare minimum—reading assigned essays only once and then very quickly, cranking out a first draft in record time at the last minute and then going over it only once or twice to fix spelling and formatting, etc. —then you should not expect your writing to improve much at all by the end of the semester. But if you do put significant time into your work, you will likely see improvement.

How much time are we talking about? The standard calculation is that you should budget two hours out of class for every hour in class. Thus, if you are in class 4 hours each week, you should be spending 8 hours out of class each week on the course work. This means reading, annotating, drafting, reviewing, and so on. You also need to do the same for the other classes you are taking. If you are overloaded at school, at work and with other obligations, you will likely find that you are not performing as well as you could, so consider cutting back where you can.

Here's another way to look at it. Think of something you've learned to do well—playing an instrument, excelling at a sport, performing in a play, dancing, cooking, etc. Whatever the skill, you didn't get good at it by reading about what to do. Instead, you practiced. You can study a playbook as part of a football team, or look at a music book as you learn to play the guitar, but those things won't help you when the ball is snapped or when you turn on your amplifier. Drilling with your teammates or forcing your fingers to find the notes on the guitar over and over will be the only way to improve.

Writing works the same way. You can read everything in this book, and it won't necessarily make you a better writer. Instead, you need to drill and practice, write and re-write. After working at it for a while—weeks, months, whole semesters—your writing will be stronger than it was when you started. Without practice, though, your progress will be much slower.

A Note About English Teachers Or 2+2=5

One frustrating thing for students in English classes is that English tends to be rather subjective. That is, the standards for what makes "good" writing may vary from instructor to instructor. In your math classes, you can count on some things being constant: two plus two always equals four, for instance. Different math instructors may have different requirements for showing your work or may use different methods to solve problems, but the standards for what makes a correct answer generally don't change. In English, that's not always the case. You may be coming into this class having been taught, for example, that a thesis can only be one sentence long or that it MUST contain a word like "because." You may also have been taught to write in standard 5-paragraph essay format (more on this later). In this class, you may learn an entirely new set of standards for what is correct, or "good" writing. And then, surprise! You move on to the next course in the sequence to find another instructor with a whole new set of standards. Similarly, when instructors in disciplines other than English require essays, papers and projects from you, their standards of "good" writing may also vary from what your English teacher has taught you. There are several reasons for this—instructors with different training, different emphases, instructors who teach at different colleges, etc.

One way to get around this problem is simply to ask your instructor what he or she requires and to listen closely when standards of good writing are explained in class.

Rather than get frustrated by this, try to keep focused on the idea that academic writing means writing for an audience and that different audiences have different expectations. The recipient of an email or text message expects you to use different words, a different tone of voice and even a different format than you would in writing a formal essay or an article or a letter to your Senator. Thus, the practice you get in writing to meet different instructors' expectations is actually helping you to develop as a writer. You are, in effect, adding more tools to your writer's toolbox.

Where Do We Go From Here?

In the rest of this guide, you will find advice on how to get the most out of your reading, how to use the writing process to help you generate strong material, how to organize your work effectively, and how to avoid common errors in grammar and usage. Some of this material may be new to you, and some may be review; regardless, you will likely find that following the advice in this guide will lead to improvements in your writing if you apply it and put the advice to work.

Chapter One: Active Reading

Getting the Most out of What You Read

Many students approach reading in a way that is not always productive. They assume that the author of a text is the expert and that they—the readers—know very little about the topic. It is as though the students view themselves as sponges waiting to absorb the material in the text. They are reading passively, expecting the writer and the text to do all the work, to transfer meaning into the readers' minds as if by magic.

The problem with this approach is that such students do not consider the knowledge, experience and insight that *they can bring to the text*. Without a reader, a book or an article is nothing but ink and paper; a website is nothing but computer code designed to look like words and images. These things require readers for them to have meaning, and the most productive and effective way for this to happen is for students to become active readers.

Active reading involves several steps:

- Previewing the text
- Annotating the text
- Reflecting on the text

Previewing the Text. When you go to the movies, you often make your choice of which film to see based on previews you have seen. The previews give you a sense of what type of movie it will be: action, comedy, adventure, drama, etc. It helps you know what to expect from the film before you pay your money and sit down in the theater.

Previewing a text can give you the same sort of insight when you read. Rather than approach a text not knowing what it will contain, if you take a few minutes to preview it, you will have a sense of where the author is going, what the main ideas are, etc. before you start the actual reading. This will help you get more meaning out of your reading.

To preview a text, you should first read any introductory material that is provided. Introductions can give you a sense of who the author is, what else he or she has written or how the author is an expert on the subject. You can also get a sense of when the piece was written and any other pertinent information. Next, take a moment to read over the subheadings in the piece, if there are any. These will give you a sense of how the text is organized and what the author's main points are. If there are no subheadings, read the first paragraph (looking for the text's main idea) and then the first sentences of each paragraph that follows. You should also carefully read the final paragraph to see the author's final thoughts.

Annotating the text. When you are finished previewing the text, read it carefully with a pen or pencil in hand. This is not the same as reading with a highlighter. When you highlight or underline, you are noting things that strike you as important, but you may not remember why you thought this when you go back to look at the text later. Instead, using a pen or pencil, **write notes in the margins** about:

- Main ideas
- Key supporting points
- Things the author says that you find particularly effective
- Things the author says that you do not understand or don't agree with
- Anything else that strikes you as important or interesting

Put **brackets** around key terms or sentences rather than underlining.

You can also make **question marks** in the margins next to passages you have difficulty with. This way, if your instructor asks if anyone has questions about the reading, you can go straight to your question marks and get some answers rather than having to skim through the reading, looking for the things that confused you when you first read the text.

Finally, you should **circle vocabulary words** whose meanings are unclear to you. When you have finished reading, look up the words in a good dictionary and **write the definitions** in the margins of the text you annotated. While this may seem like a lot of extra work, the simple fact is that if you do

Annotation Toolbox

- Write notes in the margins
- Use [brackets] rather than underlining to set off key points
- Use ??? in the margins to help remember things you have questions about
- Circle vocabulary words and write definitions in the margins

not understand the words in a text, you will not get as much out of it as you could or should. Someone reading T.C. Boyle's short story "Greasy Lake" would see that he uses the word "testudineous" to describe a character

crawling on the ground in the middle of a fight. A reader who fails to look this word up in a dictionary would miss out on the fact that it means "being like a turtle" and would thus not fully understand what the story's narrator is describing. Looking up words you are unfamiliar with will increase your understanding of what you have read and will also help you to build your vocabulary.

See page 8 for an example of an annotated text.

Reflecting on the Text. Once you have finished reading and annotating, take a few minutes to write a journal entry. This should be an informal response to what you have read, a chance for you to record your thoughts about the text, its main ideas, organization, examples and language. You should also take the time to record your thoughts on what the author did well and anything you think the author could have done a better job with. Try to emulate in your own writing the things the author did well and avoid the sort of writing you found unsuccessful.

Time Consuming…But Worth It

Reading actively does take more time than just quickly reading through your assignments one time. However, you will find that if you devote more time to reading, you will get more out of the material. Your writing will also begin to improve if you pay careful attention to what you read. Additionally, if you have carefully and actively read your assignments in preparation for class, you will find that you are more engaged with the material and better prepared to participate in discussions and activities.

Here is an annotated page from *Narrative of the Life of Frederick Douglass, an American Slave*:

> stratagems= strategies
>
> The mistress started out teaching him but stopped
>
> Morally corrupt
>
> She had to be trained to treat him badly.

I lived in Master Hugh's family about seven years. During this time, I succeeded in learning to read and write. In accomplishing this, I was compelled to resort to various stratagems. I had no regular teacher. My mistress, who had kindly commenced to instruct me, had, in compliance with the advice and direction of her husband, not only ceased to instruct, but had set her face against my being instructed by any one else. It is due, however, to my mistress to say of her, that she did not adopt this course of treatment immediately. She at first lacked the depravity indispensable to shutting me up in mental darkness. It was at least necessary for her to have some training in the exercise of irresponsible power, to make her equal to the task of treating me as though I were a brute.

> What does he mean by simplicity?
>
> — that he was her property
>
> Harmful
>
> Interesting – slavery is as harmful to the slave owner as it is to the slave. Is this really true?
>
> — take away from
>
> Rules

My mistress was, as I have said, a kind and tender-hearted woman; and in the simplicity of her soul she commenced, when I first went to live with her, to treat me as she supposed one human being ought to treat another. In entering upon the duties of a slaveholder, she did not seem to perceive that I sustained to her the relation of a mere chattel, and that for her to treat me as a human being was not only wrong, but dangerously so. Slavery proved as injurious to her as it did to me. When I went there, she was a pious, warm, and tender-hearted woman. There was no sorrow or suffering for which she had not a tear. She had bread for the hungry, clothes for the naked, and comfort for every mourner that came within her reach. Slavery soon proved its ability to divest her of these heavenly qualities. Under its influence, the tender heart became stone, and the lamblike disposition gave way to one of tiger-like fierceness. The first step in her downward course was in her ceasing to instruct me. She now commenced to practise her husband's precepts. She finally became even more violent in her opposition than her husband himself. She was not satisfied with simply doing as well as he had commanded; she seemed anxious to do better. Nothing seemed to make her more angry than to see me with a newspaper. She seemed to think that here lay the danger. I have had her rush at me with a face made all up of fury, and snatch from me a newspaper, in a manner that fully revealed her apprehension. She was an apt woman; and a little experience soon demonstrated, to her satisfaction, that education and slavery were incompatible with each other.

> What was so bad about teaching slaves to read?
>
> intelligent – a good learner.

After completing this annotation, the student could proceed by writing a journal entry on the significance of Douglass' argument about the effects of slavery on the slave and on the slaveholder. The annotation allows the student to explore his or her thoughts in conjunction with gaining an understanding of the material.

Your Turn

Find a brief passage of your own choosing to practice the Active Reading strategies you've learned in this chapter. It could be a short essay assigned for this class, a newspaper or magazine article, or an article you have found online (make sure you have a hard copy that you can mark up when you annotate). Choose something you find interesting and go through the steps: preview the text, annotate it, and write a short reflection about it.

Chapter Two: Invention

Writing Is a Process

Another common misconception among student writers is that good writers are people who can sit down in front of a blank piece of paper or open a new file in their word processor and turn out a perfectly executed essay or article on their first try. As noted in the introduction, this is not how most writers write, and even those who appear to be able to do this are likely taking the time to shape and polish the work in their minds before ever putting a word on paper or screen. Instead, almost anyone who writes successfully and effectively treats writing as a process involving several steps:

- Invention (also called pre-writing)
- Drafting
- Revision
- Proofreading and Editing

In this chapter, we will examine the first step in this process.

Here's My Assignment. Now What Do I Do?

In a perfect world, we would only need to write about things we find interesting and already know a lot about. When someone writes a diary entry about the things he or she did on a given day, the words usually flow easily and quickly because the subject is familiar; the writer is comfortable describing his or her day.

Unfortunately, in academic writing, you are usually asked to write about things you are only learning about. Sometimes, the topics you are assigned will not be things you are immediately interested in. This makes it harder to write, harder to get those ideas onto a piece of paper or a blank computer screen. If you're pressuring yourself to get it right the first time (or if you've waited until the last minute to start your essay), then the task becomes even more difficult.

Instead of putting pressure on yourself to churn out a perfectly executed paper on a topic you have not given much thought to, you should engage in the process of **discovering** or **inventing** your thoughts on the subject. There are several strategies you can employ, including

- Freewriting
- Listing (or brainstorming)
- Clustering
- Asking Questions

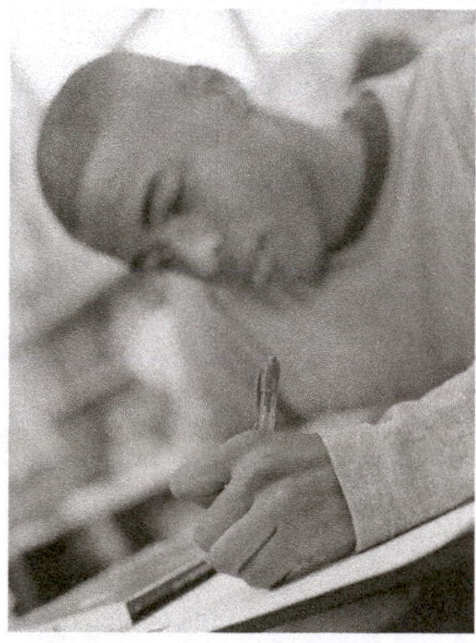

You can use these techniques to help you narrow your topic. If an instructor assigns a Remembered Event essay and gives little other guidelines, a student can use invention strategies to determine what moment from his or her past would be the best to focus on in writing the essay.

Once you have determined what you are going to write about, use invention to help you gather material that will eventually grow into an essay. In this form, the material is rough, and you need to keep in mind that this kind of writing is extremely informal. You should not be concerned with what is correct or incorrect, whether you are generating strong or weak material, or about your grammar and spelling being correct or incorrect. At this point, writing is not about right and wrong. It is just about getting ideas out of your head and onto a piece of paper or computer file where they can be preserved and worked with later.

Different writers will find some methods more appealing or useful than others. Try experimenting with different invention strategies to see what works best for you.

Freewriting. When you freewrite, you give yourself a time limit and a specific topic. With a blank sheet of paper or a new file opened on your computer, write non-stop on your topic. If you make mistakes, keep going. If you use the wrong word, keep going. If you run out of ideas, find a way to continue—even if it means writing "I'm running out of ideas. I'm running out of ideas" until something else occurs to you. The point is that your pen should not leave the paper. If you're typing, your fingers should not leave the keyboard. Write, and write, and write some more until you have reached the time limit you set for yourself—usually ten minutes.

When you have completed your freewrite, read it over, circling any ideas that strike you as interesting or worthy of further exploration. Write one of those ideas at the top of a new sheet of paper or in a new file on the computer and do another freewrite. After doing this three or four times, you will have generated quite a bit of material that you can then begin shaping into paragraphs in your first draft. Keep in mind that much of the material in your freewrite will be discarded as you begin shaping your draft. The goal is not to start writing at this stage but rather to discover what you want to write about and what you want to say about your subject.

Here is a sample freewrite. The student has been assigned to write on a rite of passage and its significance.

> I suppose I've been through a lot of rites of passage. It's hard to know what the most significant one has been. I could write about graduation or getting my driver's license. But those seem so typical. I could also write about the first day I went to work. The first day of college would be good, too. I remember how nervous I was. The first day I went to college, I was shocked at how crowded the parking lot was. There was nowhere to park, and the line of cars going into the parking lot was worse than anytime I've gone to Disneyland or a concert. Then I had to find my first class. I had a map of the campus and was walking around with it, trying not to look like I was lost. I remember when I was a freshman in high school; everybody had maps of the campus then, too. They were printed in bright red on the backs of folders the administration gave out. It was easy to spot

the freshman because we all had those red maps. On my first day of college, I didn't want to look like that, like I was new and confused. Even though I was. There was something about being a college student that said I was supposed to be different, an adult now. I didn't feel like an adult. I didn't feel any different than I had the summer before, I mean three months before when I had graduated high school. The idea that graduation was supposed to have changed me was kind of a joke. I didn't even know what I was doing in college or why I was there. I just went because it seemed like I was expected to. Why was I there? I suppose if I had really known what I was doing, I would have gone to the campus before the first day, not just to register. I would have looked up where my classes were and found out about parking. I would have done a lot of things differently. The thing is, when I think about that day now, I don't really remember what happened in the first class. I know what it was and who the teacher was and which building it was in, but what happened in the class? Can I really write about this when I don't know everything that happened? I think I can. I know I only had one class that day, and it seemed to be full of people who knew exactly what they were doing. It took me a long time to feel like I belonged.

As you can see, this is very rough and does not really qualify as a paragraph, as it is poorly organized and unfocused. But freewriting is not about organization or focus. The student writing this has discovered a few things about the first day of college and could likely take some of the key elements of this freewrite—the sense of feeling lost, trying to hide it, the desire to find a sense of place—and develop them into an essay about how the first day of college helped shape the student into a different person.

Listing. When you list (or brainstorm), you basically do the same thing as when you freewrite. You give yourself a topic and a time limit, but instead of writing sentences, you simply list as many ideas and details as you can think of. Again, don't censor yourself. Write down everything that comes to mind, paying no attention to spelling or whether the ideas you're listing are promising or not. Here is a sample listing activity by a student trying to develop some ideas for an essay on popular culture.

Beatles songs	Movies
Yesterday	Help
Revolution	Yellow Submarine
Helter Skelter	Drugs
Imagine	Influence?
John Lennon, not Beatles	Music
Imagine there's no heaven	Culture
Communist?	40 years later
Beatlemania	Still listening
Long hair	Still popular
Ed Sullivan show	Why?
Screaming teenagers	Strawberry fields
Why'd they break up?	Childhood

Ideas in this list could be developed into an essay about the Beatles and their influence, possibly exploring the reasons their music has had a lasting impact or else explaining how it was different from music of other artists from the same time period.

Clustering. This invention strategy may be more useful for students who think and learn more visually than verbally. It is a graphic way of recording your thoughts. Start by writing your topic in the center of a page and circle it. Write down the first thing that comes to mind about your topic, circling this also and drawing a line between the two circles. Working with the second circle, extend the network of ideas, circles and lines as far out as you can. When you run out of ideas, work your way back to the center, coming up with new ideas and extending the clusters in other directions.

Here is a cluster for an essay exploring the difficulties faced by first-generation college students.

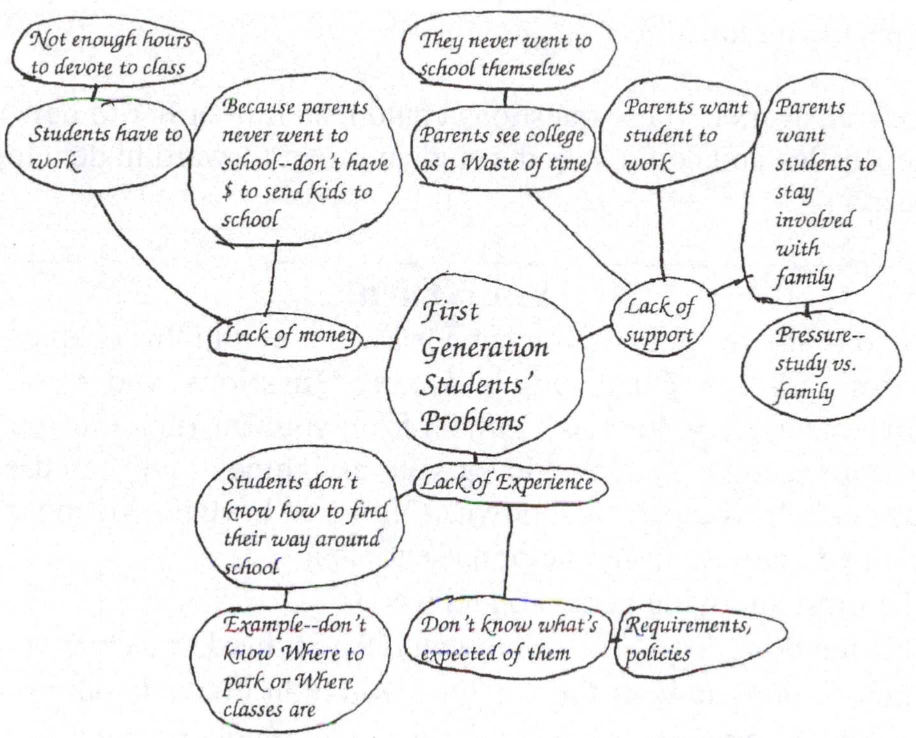

When you have filled a page, you can look at the different groupings of ideas. Thinking about how each cluster could form a paragraph or a section of your paper, you can begin organizing your essay and turning the material in the cluster into sentences.

Asking Questions. Another method of inventing material to include in an essay is to ask questions about your subject and then answer them. Start with the basics—Who? What? Where? When? Why? How? Then move on to ask more probing questions. The student working on the Beatles essay could ask him or herself the following:

- Who was influenced by the Beatles?
- What were some of the things that made them different from other bands?
- Where were they most popular?
- When was their influence at its greatest?
- Why are they still so popular?
- How have other groups or musicians borrowed from Beatles music?
- Would the Beatles succeed if they were still recording today?

- How did they change the culture?
- How did they change music?
- Did they change the way people listen to music, the things people expect from music?

A student's answers to these questions could lead him or her to new ideas about the Beatles and could help the student move forward in developing his or her essay.

Your Turn

Choose two of the techniques you have learned about in this chapter (**Freewriting, Listing, Clustering** or **Asking Questions**) and try them out. If you already have a writing assignment from your instructor, use that topic. If you are struggling to find a topic for your assignment, you can use these techniques to help you narrow it down. Or, if you have no writing assignment yet, choose from one of these topics:

- The most annoying person on television
- The one thing in your life you would find it hardest to live without
- The one thing in your life you wish you didn't have to put up with
- The one thing you wish the older generation understood about you and your friends

Remember that Invention is really just for you, so don't worry about being correct, using perfect grammar or effective word choice. The point is just to get your ideas down on paper. You'll work on polishing your ideas later.

Now What?

Once you have generated several pages of invention or discovery, you are ready to begin developing your first draft. Remember, however, that the writing process is not a one-way street. If you find that you run out of ideas while drafting, return to your invention strategies, generating more material to help you move forward in your draft.

As with active reading, you will find that the more time you put into this part of the writing process, the more productive your work will be in later stages.

Chapter Three: Organizing and Drafting

Putting It All Together

Now that you have decided on a topic for your essay and have generated some ideas about it, it's time to start putting your ideas together in essay format. This means that you need to begin thinking about your work on a more formal level, and there are several things you need to consider. These include your essay's

- Audience
- Thesis
- Paragraphs

These elements add up to give your essay some form of **Organization**. There will likely be many different ways you can organize your work, and you will likely be better off if you give yourself plenty of time to experiment.

Who Am I Writing For?
Or
For Whom Am I Writing?

One of the key elements that any writer should consider is the written text's intended audience. If you are writing a journal or diary entry, you probably

don't pay much attention to spelling or grammar. Since you are your own audience in this case, it is doubtful that you will concern yourself with how closely you follow the rules. If someone is writing a text message or an email to a friend, the writer will likely use abbreviations like "u" for "you" or "2day" for "today." However, if the email is to a business associate, the language will likely be a bit more formal, as the writer will be considering the needs of his or her audience and may be concerned that the email's recipient will judge the writer's professionalism or intelligence based on the content of the written message.

While writing an essay for an academic audience, you need to be aware that your readers have certain expectations. These include the level of language you use, your attention to detail, the development of your paragraphs, and the presence of a clear, insightful thesis. Your ability to follow grammar conventions is also crucial, as this will help you to communicate your ideas effectively and efficiently.

For all practical purposes, the audience most students care about is their professor. You should be aware, however, that most professors stress that their students should be writing for a well-informed, general public audience, some members of which may not agree with what the student has written. It may help you to think of your peers in this class as your audience or to imagine yourself writing for a reasonably well-educated person whom you respect and whose interest you want to hold.

The Thesis

Arguably, the thesis is the most important part of your essay. Other texts may refer to the thesis as the controlling idea, the dominant theme, a roadmap to the essay, etc. In short, your thesis is your main idea, and you need to think carefully about how you are going to express it.

Before thinking about the qualities of a good thesis, it might be helpful to think about what a thesis should *not* do:

1. **It should not be a question.** Often, students are tempted to write a short introductory paragraph that ends with a question, and their plan is to let the body paragraphs answer the question. In a History class, having a thesis like *What were the main causes of World War I?* would not work well since the student doesn't really present his or her own ideas on the subject but rather lets the reader know that the following paragraphs will basically amount to a list of causes and effects. When you ask your reader a question, the reader tries to answer it, and when your thesis is a question, you are basically giving control of the essay over to the reader, allowing him or her to answer the question. If the answer that your paper then delivers differs from the reader's expectation, you may have lost the reader entirely.
2. **It should not be a simple statement of fact.** A thesis ought to be something that is arguable or in need of explanation. A thesis like *Driving slower leads to better fuel economy* doesn't really need explanation or support, and whatever the writer includes after this will not likely be very interesting to a reader.

3. **It should not list your supporting points.** Having a thesis that lists supporting points is typical of the 5-paragraph essay (more on this later) that many of you were taught to write and rely on. The listing thesis looks like this: *The legal drinking age should be lowered to 18 because that is the age required for voting, for joining the armed forces and for purchasing other restricted items like firearms and tobacco.* It's not a bad thesis so much as it's a bit boring. This is something you'll need to work on avoiding since it's a bit too formulaic and basic. It can get the job done in the short term, but if you want to advance as a writer, drop those listing thesis statements.
4. **It should not be boring.** No one likes to be bored. We feel almost tortured when listening to a boring storyteller or being stuck watching a boring film. Your readers feel the same when your thesis is boring. It tells them that the rest of the essay will likely be boring, too. If you can imagine a reader saying, "Who cares?" in response to your thesis, try to find a more interesting way of saying it.
5. **It should not simply be an announcement of the topic.** Your reader already knows that you've written an essay, so you don't need to write *This essay will be about drinking and driving.* Instead, let the reader know what you're going to *say* about drinking and driving rather than making the reader wait until halfway through the essay to see your point.

Instead of having a thesis that commits the sins we've just outlined, it will be far better to write a thesis that has the following traits:

1. **It needs to identify the essay's topic.**
2. **It needs to present the topic as something that is arguable or in need of explanation.**
3. **It needs to express the writer's point of view on the topic.**
4. **It needs to give the reader some sense of what the point of view is based on.**
5. **It needs to use specific language.**
6. **It needs to respond directly to the writing assignment, question or prompt.**

It's one thing to list all the qualities of an effective thesis, and another to develop a thesis that does all those things. If you've been used to writing thesis statements that fall into any of the "Don't Do This" categories above, then getting your thesis statements into shape for college-level essays is going to take some work. Don't get frustrated. Like anything else explained in this book, you will get better at it only if you work at it; your first attempt at writing a solid thesis for your paper probably won't be as successful as you'd like. It's more important that you try and that you not give up.

Quick Thesis Checklist	
A good thesis will: ✓ Identify the essay's topic ✓ Present the author's point of view as something arguable or in need of explanation ✓ Give the reader a sense of what the point of view is based on ✓ Be Specific ✓ Address the prompt	A good thesis won't: ✗ Be phrased as a question ✗ Simply state a fact ✗ Simply list supporting points ✗ Be boring ✗ Be a simple announcement of your topic

You should keep in mind that your thesis will likely go through several stages. In fact, it *should* go through several stages. The version you start with is not usually the best you can come up with. At this point, you may not have a strong sense of where the whole draft is going, so why lock yourself into a thesis so early in the process? Think of your first attempt as a **working thesis** and then come back to polish it a bit more. Your working thesis should simply and directly identify the topic and what you think about it—like this:

Snakes make good pets.	*This working thesis identifies the topic* (snakes) *and gives the reader a sense of what the writer thinks about the topic* (they make good pets).

The writer of a paper on this subject could develop the thesis in a variety of ways as the essay takes shape:

Keeping a pet snake can be enriching for a pet owner.	*This thesis is taking shape in the sense that it uses more specific language* (enriching) *rather than the generic term the writer started with* (good).
While some people fear snakes, the person who keeps a snake as a pet will likely find it an enriching experience. Allowing a captive snake to thrive may be challenging, but the rewards are great, as the pet owner can enjoy his or her fascinating, beautiful and somewhat mysterious companion for many years.	*This thesis is more specific, explaining how snake ownership can be enriching* (rewarding in spite of or because of the challenge; snakes offer lasting companionship; great enjoyment can come from snake ownership). *It also presents the topic as arguable by noting an opposing view* (people's fear of snakes) *that the essay will presumably work against.*

Your Turn

Group Activity: Get into groups of 3-4 students. Everyone should have paper and pen or pencil. As a group, decide on one of the following topics:

- Facebook
- Mixed Martial Arts
- Lowering the Legal Drinking Age
- Making Your College a Smoke-Free Campus

Each person in the group should write his or her own rough working thesis, just a sentence or two in which you try to express your opinion about the topic. Once everyone is finished, trade papers with someone in your group.

All group members should consider the characteristics of strong thesis statements outlined in this chapter and then work on revising their partner's working thesis. Once everyone is finished, trade papers again and revise further. Your goal is to polish and strengthen the thesis statements to make them as strong as possible.

Repeat the activity until each group member has his/her original thesis again. Compare the revised thesis to the original working thesis you started with.

Saying Goodbye to the 5-paragraph Essay

You may have been taught to write what is called the 5-paragraph essay. You may really like writing this type of essay, as it's dependable and predictable. Once you master it, you can use it for all sorts of writing situations. There was a time when this was the accepted standard of college-level composition courses. Those times, however, have changed, and the 5-paragraph essay these days is generally considered too basic, too formulaic and too limiting. The 5-paragraph essay may be useful to teach students that their essays need to be clearly structured, but after that it becomes a crutch, and many students begin to feel that the 5-paragraph essay is the *only* way to structure their essays. As a result, they miss out on opportunities to expand their ideas and to explore relationships between ideas that they might not have been open to if locked into the old formula of five paragraphs.

Here's the way a 5-paragraph essay on the snake topic above might be structured.

Paragraph 1 Introduction with a thesis that reads, "Snakes make good pets because they are challenging, fascinating and beautiful."

Paragraph 2 This is the first body paragraph and would give examples about how challenging it is to properly keep pet snakes.

Paragraph 3 This is the second body paragraph and would give examples about how fascinating snakes are.

Paragraph 4 This is the third body paragraph and would describe how beautiful snakes are.

Paragraph 5 This would be the conclusion, usually little more than a summary.

A bit boring, isn't it? Instead of locking oneself into this tired old formula, an academic writer would be far better off developing an essay around the thesis we arrived at earlier. But how? If you've been used to writing 5-paragraph essays, the paragraph topics are pretty easily laid out for you. In getting away from this formula, though, you'll find yourself having to do a bit more work in the planning stage. It's worth it, however. The resulting essays will be much stronger and more interesting for your reader.

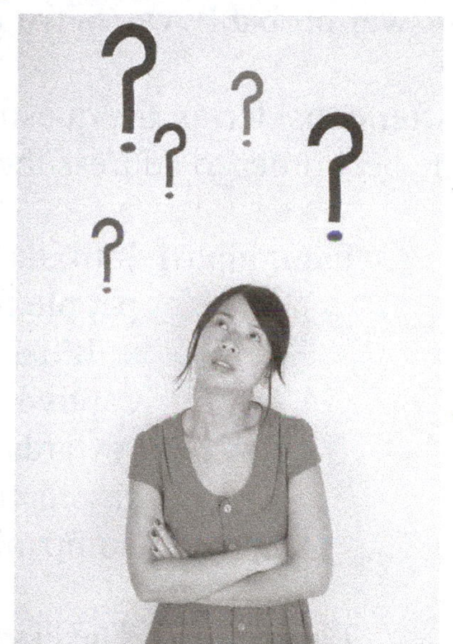

And your reader, by the way, is of great importance at this point. Once you arrive at a thesis, you should stop and do some more Invention/Discovery, trying to get into your reader's head. Ask yourself: *what questions will my reader have after seeing this thesis?* Your answers should point the way toward the topics for your body paragraphs. Remember that the body paragraphs need to **support the thesis**, and that support will not be achieved if the reader is left with too many unanswered questions by the end of the essay.

So, after doing some quick brainstorming, a writer might come up with this list of possible questions that a reader might be left with after seeing the thesis about snakes:

How common is it for people to keep pet snakes?
Why are people afraid of snakes, anyway?
How, exactly, are snakes "enriching"?
Do people keep poisonous snakes?
Why is it challenging to keep a pet snake?
What makes the author such an expert on snakes?
What's wrong with just having dogs and cats?
What's so special about snakes?
How long do snakes live?

Going over this list, the author could then decide which questions most need to be answered, and in what order. Some of the questions seem to fit in with others. For example, the question about poisonous snakes could be answered in the same paragraph as the one about people's fear of snakes. And the questions about snakes being special, enriching and different from dogs and cats could be answered in a paragraph focusing on the things that make snake ownership a rewarding experience.

Remember that not all the questions need to be answered, nor do they all need the same amount of space devoted to them. The question on how long snakes live, for instance, might not need to be answered at all since the answer probably varies from species to species.

After considering the questions, grouping them together, and thinking about the best order to address them, a student might come up with this outline:

Paragraph 1 Introduction with the following thesis: While some people fear snakes, the person who keeps a snake as a pet will likely find it an enriching experience. Allowing a captive snake to thrive may be challenging, but the rewards are great, as the pet owner can enjoy his or her fascinating, beautiful and somewhat mysterious companion for many years.

Paragraph 2 The essay's first body paragraph could explore people's fear of snakes, perhaps giving examples about poisonous snakes or even using the snake in the story of the Garden of Eden as an example.

Paragraph 3 The next body paragraph could begin the discussion of pet snakes, perhaps using some personal experience to show how the author has come to his or her understanding of snakes.

Paragraph 4 This body paragraph could go into detail on the challenges of snake ownership—suitable enclosures, heat sources, feeding, handling a snake, etc.

Paragraph 5 In this body paragraph, the author could explain the benefits to be had when the challenges in paragraph 4 are met, perhaps using examples of what a snake owner can learn about nature or how he or she can come to a greater appreciation for the beauty of exotic animals.

Paragraph 6 In the essay's conclusion, the author would provide his or her final thoughts on the issue of keeping pet snakes, possibly referring back to the issues brought up in the introduction but doing more than summarizing the essay's main points.

As you can see, breaking away from the 5-paragraph model opens a world of possibilities for the writer, allowing him or her to explore topics and provide a range of supporting points to make the essay more interesting and much more fully developed.

If Not Five Paragraphs, Then What?

Cut loose from the traditional 5-paragraph essay, some students are left wondering just how they should organize their work. The answer is that your essay's organization will depend on a variety of factors, including the topic, the assignment, and the needs of your audience. In some cases, you will be given specific guidelines for constructing your essay.

You may be asked to write a **narrative** essay, in which case you will likely organize your essay **chronologically**, or in the order that events happened in time.

You may be asked to write an **expository** essay in which you explain something—a concept, a phenomenon, a condition, etc. In this case, you will likely need to use some form of **logical** organization, perhaps moving from **general to specific** or from **specific to general** depending on the needs of your audience. You may also want to organize your supporting points in order of **importance** or **interest**. If you are **comparing** or **contrasting** two subjects and making a point about their similarities or differences, you will need to go back and forth between your subjects in a logical, orderly manner. In the essay on snakes outlined above, the body paragraphs are organized to focus on the audience's likely predisposition toward snakes, followed by more specific paragraphs explaining the author's experience with reptiles, the needs of snakes, and the rewards to be gained from properly caring for them. In other words, the essay moves from general to specific and also puts the subjects that are likely of most interest to the audience in the first and last body paragraphs. The writer assumes that readers will likely identify with the material in the first body paragraph about people's fear of snakes and with the sense of satisfaction and enrichment that comes from doing something well, which is a rather common sensation regardless of what one is getting satisfaction from. The paragraphs on the proper care of snakes and the author's personal experiences with snakes may be of less interest to the reader, so they are placed in the middle of the essay in the areas of least **emphasis**.

You may also be asked to write an **argumentative** essay in which your focus is to persuade your reader of your point of view on a specific subject. Here, you would also want to organize your essay **logically**, taking into consideration your audience's needs as you would with the expository essay. However, in the persuasive essay, you would also need to include **opposing ideas** and argue against them. It is possible to organize an argumentative essay entirely around a series of opposing ideas and the author's contrasting views.

There will be more later on each of these methods of organizing your essays.

Let's Talk about Paragraphs

At some point, many student writers are told that a paragraph is supposed to be a specific number of sentences in length. As with being taught to write the 5-paragraph essay, this sort of thing is used as writing instruction to get students to perform a specific task—in this case, developing their paragraphs. But also like the 5-paragraph essay, the "rule" that paragraphs must be a specific length is arbitrary and artificial and should not be followed as you develop your writing more fully. A paragraph can be any length—from one sentence to more than a hundred. It just depends on the subject being written about. Some are complex, and others are simple. Develop your paragraphs accordingly.

There are, however, some definite rules of paragraph development that ought to be followed:

- Paragraphs are unified.
- Paragraphs are coherent.

- Paragraphs are developed.
- Paragraphs should say something of substance.

Paragraphs Are Unified. Unity in paragraphs simply means that everything in a paragraph is related to a single idea. When you've written everything you need to write about that idea, it's time to move on to the next main idea in a new paragraph. Doing this effectively requires the writer to know what a paragraph's main idea is. If you're starting new paragraphs because it just seems like one is needed, you're probably not organizing your essay effectively. Go back and give it some more thought. You should be able to say what the main idea is in each one of your paragraphs, and you should be certain that your instructor will also be looking for the main idea. If it can't be found, there's a problem. If there is anything in the paragraph that gets off the subject, then the paragraph is lacking unity. Delete the stray material, move it into a new paragraph, or re-think the paragraph's main idea to incorporate the new material more smoothly.

Another element of unity is that most paragraphs have a **topic sentence**. Just as the thesis is the controlling idea of the whole essay, the topic sentence is the controlling idea of an individual paragraph. Typically, the topic sentence is the first sentence in a paragraph and will be the most general piece of information. It will be followed by specific examples and explanations of those examples that show how the examples are supporting the topic sentence. Be aware, however, that some paragraphs, especially in narrative essays, may not have clearly identifiable topic sentences; regardless, each paragraph will always have a clear point, a main idea that is related to the thesis and is developed in the paragraph through examples and explanations.

Here is an example of a paragraph lacking unity:

Topic Sentence

It might be accurate to describe Link Wray as an accidental guitar innovator, years ahead of his time. One night in the late

Example and explanation of how it relates to the topic sentence.

1950s, while playing a dance with his band The Wray Men, Wray received a request from the audience for a song that he did not know. Not wanting to disappoint, he improvised, banging out an instrumental that closely approximated the requested song but with a sound all its own. The resulting effort became "Rumble," the first song ever banned from radio play because of its implied violence and, perhaps more significantly, the first rock instrumental to employ what would later become known as the "power chord." This style would later be copied by the Kinks and many other bands in the 1960s and 70s. *Wray focused so much on playing the guitar because he had lost a lung to tuberculosis, and doctors had told him he would not be able to sing. He proved them wrong, however, and the resulting rawness in his vocals as he was practically gasping for air gave his songs a desperate tone, making them seem like early punk rock.* After his success with "Rumble," Wray went on to other guitar innovations, effectively inventing distortion by using a pencil to poke holes in the speaker cone of his amplifier—a sound future musicians would achieve with electronics. Even the energy of his music foreshadowed that of later artists; indeed, club owners begged him not to play "Run, Chicken, Run," as the song's tempo inevitably inspired listeners to get into brawls reminiscent of today's mosh pits.

The italicized sentences are off-topic, about Wray's vocal style, not guitar innovations.

If the italicized sentences in this paragraph were removed, the paragraph would be unified. Note that the material need not be completely discarded but could be used as an example in another paragraph about the musician's vocal style and innovation.

Paragraphs Are Coherent. For a paragraph to be coherent, there must be clear connections between the ideas in it. Coherence is achieved through **repetition of key terms** and **transitional phrases**. Most often, writers include these things automatically or instinctively when they compose paragraphs. Even so, you should pay attention to the way your ideas are connected, keeping in mind that your main job in writing is to communicate your ideas effectively to your reader.

For example, we can look at the paragraph above, clearly unified now. The words in **bold** give the paragraph coherence:

> It might be accurate to describe **Link Wray** as an accidental **guitar innovator**, years ahead of his time. **One night** in the late 1950s, while playing a dance with **his** band The Wray Men, **Wray** received a request from the audience for a **song** that **he** did not know. Not wanting to disappoint, **he** improvised, banging out an **instrumental** that closely approximated the requested **song** but with a **sound all its**

> **own**. **The resulting effort** became "Rumble," the first **song** ever banned from radio play because of **its** implied violence and, perhaps more significantly, the first rock instrumental to employ what would later become known as the "**power chord**." The Kinks and other more recent bands like Green Day would later **copy this style**. **After his** success with "Rumble," **Wray** went on to other guitar **innovations**, effectively inventing **distortion** by using a pencil to poke holes in the speaker cone of **his** amplifier—a sound future musicians would achieve with electronics. **Even** the energy of **his** music **foreshadowed** that of later artists; **indeed**, club owners begged **him** not to play "Run, Chicken, Run," as the **song's** tempo inevitably inspired listeners to get into brawls reminiscent of today's mosh pits.

Note that every sentence has some reference either to Link Wray (or a pronoun referring to him) or to the innovations in his songs. There are also transitional words and phrases ("the resulting effort," "rather," "even," "indeed") to make connections from one example to the next and between examples and the main idea.

Paragraphs Are Developed. As noted above, a paragraph needs either a clearly stated topic sentence or an unstated but equally clear main idea. Assuming that your audience needs more information to understand fully the paragraph's main idea, the writer needs to develop his or her paragraph with detailed examples and explanations of them. The paragraph above about Link Wray is fully developed. It starts off with a general statement about its subject and follows it with specific examples and explanations, naming musicians, songs and innovations to help a reader understand what is meant by the topic sentence.

Paragraphs Should Say Something of Substance. This may seem like the most obvious and necessary element of a paragraph, but too often developing writers focus only on the technical aspects of paragraphs (unity, coherence, development) without giving enough thought to a paragraph's contents. For a paragraph to have substance, it needs to have something interesting to say, not something dull, not something the reader has encountered dozens of times before. Good paragraphs develop ideas and give the reader something to think about. Consider the following:

> People who read science fiction do so for a variety of reasons. Some read it strictly for entertainment; for them, there is nothing more fun

than laser fights with robots and heroes in space who are nothing more than slightly disguised cowboys. These are called "Space Operas," and the Star Wars series stands as a good example. Other people read science fiction more seriously, looking for the message that the writer may be trying to send about science or society today and where it will likely lead in the future. This is very traditional science fiction, the type of thing H.G. Wells and Jules Verne wrote in the late 1800s. Still others prefer what is called "Hard" science fiction and look at this type of writing to see how technology is employed as part of the plot; for these readers, if technology is not integral to the story and described realistically and accurately, then it may as well be a Western set in space. Regardless of why people read it, the fact remains that the genre is incredibly popular and has been for more than a hundred years now; its supporters range from the casual to the fanatical, and they show no signs of decreasing in numbers, as science fiction clearly offers something different and appealing for all of them.

This paragraph has all of the technical elements that a paragraph needs. It has a topic sentence (the first sentence). It is unified, all of the sentences relating to the main idea. It is coherent with properly placed keywords and transitions. And it is developed with sufficient examples and explanations. However, it is also rather boring, amounting to little more than a list of who reads science fiction and why. There is no real substance here, and many students are guilty of writing this way because they are preoccupied with getting their paragraphs "right" in the technical sense and forget that their paragraphs need to be *about* something.

Compare the paragraph above with this one on the same subject:

While many dismiss science fiction as juvenile entertainment or the type of books and films consumed by social misfits who keep a set of pointy plastic ears in the bottom of their sock drawer, the fact is that science fiction is by and large rather serious stuff and has been for a long time. To be sure, the genre has its fluff pieces aimed at a general audience. However, for more than a hundred years, writers of science

> fiction have been projecting into the future, into the past, into outer space and alternate worlds to make statements not about where we are going as a species but rather about where we are right now. After World War II, an awful lot of science fiction was preoccupied with the possibility of nuclear war, nuclear accidents and radiation. As personal computing became a cultural force in the 1980s and 90s, cyberpunk emerged, and its characters were average people, sometimes below average people, reflecting the shift away from technology controlled by scientists and toward technology applied and developed by everyday computer users. Indeed, in its very focus on the future, science fiction may be said to be the most optimistic of genres; even when its version of the future is dark and meant to be taken as a warning, science fiction—for the most part—still gives its fans a version of the future in which we are still here, clearly having gotten through the crises of today to be faced with new challenges in the future.

This paragraph also meets the technical requirements of paragraph writing, but it is far more interesting as the writer now has an **idea** that the paragraph is expressing and developing. This may not always be easy to achieve, but spending sufficient time in the **discovery** process of writing can help give you a sense of what you *want* to write about, not just what you think you are *supposed* to write about.

Your Turn

Look over some writing you have already done—in an essay, a rough draft, or even a journal entry—and find a paragraph that strikes you as interesting. Consider it carefully, evaluating it for Unity, Coherence, Development and Substance. In which of these areas is the paragraph weakest? Work on re-writing the paragraph to strengthen it, focusing specifically on the aspect of it that you find needs the most work. When you are done, compare the new paragraph with the original, and then see if you need to focus on any of the other three elements of successful paragraphs.

Paragraphs That Need Special Attention

It may be a cliché that we get only one chance to make a first impression, but the saying also has a measure of truth to it. The same is true of your essays: the first paragraph is probably the most important, as it gives the reader a first impression of your subject and what you are going to say about it. Similarly, the last paragraph also needs your special attention since it is the section of the essay that will give readers a final, lasting impression. So, to wrap up this section on paragraphs, we'll take a look at introductions and conclusions.

Introductions. The first paragraph of your essay is the introduction. It is, as you might guess, the section of the paper in which you introduce your reader to the topic and your point of view. When you move on to Freshman Composition and later courses, you may write more complex essays that require introductions longer than one paragraph. For now, though, let's stick to single-paragraph introductions. Your introduction should contain:

- An attention grabber, or hook
- Some general background information
- Your thesis

Think of the introduction as a funnel. It starts off wide and gets narrow as it develops. Since your audience needs to be introduced to your material, try to do something with a broad appeal to get the interest of as many readers as you can. By the time you get to your thesis, you will be expressing your own, unique perspective on the subject, but since your reader may not understand or agree or even be interested in your point of view immediately, it's best not to start with something so personal and specific. Instead, start with an attention grabber, a sentence or two that will hook the reader's interest, pulling him or her into the paragraph and preparing him or her to read your thesis.

Here are some ways you can hook your reader in the first few lines of your essay:

Ask a question
Tell a brief, interesting story
Provide a surprising or provocative fact
Use an interesting and relevant quotation

After hooking the reader, follow up with a few more sentences providing general information about the topic to give the reader a sense of perspective on the subject you are writing about. How much you write in this section of the paper will depend on a variety of things: your topic and how complex it is, your audience and what you think they know or don't know about your topic, and your purpose in writing—to explain, to argue, to narrate, etc.

Finally, your introduction should include your thesis. Most readers of academic writing expect to find your thesis at the end of your introduction. As you develop as a writer, it may be fine to work against this expectation and experiment a bit (as long as your instructor has no problem with this), but for now it is probably a good idea to stick with the expectation and place your thesis at the end of the essay's first paragraph. **Note:** You may have had previous writing instructors who referred to the first paragraph of an essay as the "thesis paragraph." Since this can confuse some students, leading them to think that the entire first paragraph is the thesis, in this guide the first paragraph will be referred to as the **introduction**, and the sentence or sentences expressing the main idea will be identified as the **thesis**.

Here is an introduction for the essay on snakes, for which we saw the thesis develop earlier:

> My grandfather won't set foot in my house. It's not because he doesn't like me, and it's not because I am a bad housekeeper. The simple fact is that my grandfather—a retired blue-collar worker and tough, no-nonsense guy—is afraid of my pet. He admits his fear is irrational, yet he has no intention of working on overcoming it. I don't have a cat or a dog or a bird or even a rat. Those things he could be around in his typical, fearless way. No, I keep a pet snake, a 7-foot long boa constrictor named Kermit, and he, in turn, keeps my grandfather away. He is not the only person to have this reaction to my choice in pets, and it is something easily understandable, as those who don't know much about snakes might not be able to tell venomous snakes from harmless ones. For others, the fact that an animal without legs can move around so well might just be plain creepy. However, while some people fear snakes, the person who keeps a snake as a pet will likely find it an enriching experience. Allowing a captive snake to thrive may be challenging, but the rewards are great, as the pet owner can enjoy his or her fascinating, beautiful and somewhat mysterious companion for many years.

Here, the hook works as a brief story, meant to be amusing by contrasting the grandfather's tough exterior with his fear of snakes. The hook is followed by some brief background establishing the writer as someone with knowledge of the subject, and the introduction ends with the thesis. The writer of this paper would then follow this introduction with the body paragraphs described earlier.

Your Turn

If you have already been assigned a topic for an essay, use that topic for this exercise. If not, look back to the topic you chose for the group exercise on thesis statements that you did on page 21. Working with your topic, write an introductory paragraph that has a **hook**, some **background information** and a **thesis statement**.

Conclusions. Some student writers mistakenly think that their essays' conclusions should be summaries of what they have written in the body paragraphs of their essays. This is not, however, what your conclusion should do. Think about it. If your essay is three to four pages long, your reader probably does not need to be reminded in the middle of page 4 of things you said on page 2. Instead of summarizing, think of your final paragraph as the place where you express your final thoughts on the subject. Remember that your introduction was like a funnel—going from general to specific. The body paragraphs have focused on the specific issues you want to write about. Now it's time to make some generalizations again, giving the reader a sense of the "big picture" ideas in your essay, thereby allowing the reader to connect with your ideas in a new way. The whole essay, then, might be said to take on something of an hourglass shape.

Here is a conclusion that could be written for the essay on pet snakes:

> A fear of snakes may be both irrational and understandable, and the same might be said of someone who loves snakes and keeps one as a pet. In a society that values kittens and

puppies, it may not make sense for a person to house a snake in his or her living room; at the same time, it makes perfect sense to the snake lover. The flicking tongue and soft scales, the determination to squeeze into the tightest of spots—all of these are things the snake lover may find endearing, and they may be made even more special in the knowledge that there are others who will never know the joys of snake ownership.

If you want, the conclusion can include a re-phrasing of the thesis, but it does not have to include this. Just as your thesis should not include a phrase like "My thesis is…" your conclusion does not need to include phrases like "in conclusion." It should be evident that this is your conclusion, so let it stand on its own. The writer who feels the need to announce that the final paragraph is the essay's conclusion reveals a lack of confidence, as though he or she fears the reader will not know that it is, in fact, the conclusion.

Just Write It

Having gone through some of the basics of organizing your draft and constructing your paragraphs, now it's time to sit down and put your draft together, moving from the rough ideas in the Invention phase to something that looks more like an essay.

When it comes right down to it, there is not much advice that can be given about the act of drafting. Writing is an action, and at some point the writer has to stop thinking and start composing. However, there are a few things you should consider:

Give Yourself Plenty of Time. If you wait until the night before your rough draft is due, you will likely be able to produce some material to turn in. However, you may also run into problems, discovering that you have not thought the material through as thoroughly as you should have and that you need to go back to the invention stage again. Before long, what little time you have left has been eaten up, and the draft you submit will not be as strong as it could have been.

Instead, budget plenty of time well before the due date. Some writers work better by doing a bit of work every day—perhaps no more than an hour. Others benefit from having a few large blocks of time of several hours to work uninterrupted. If you can schedule that kind of time a few days before the draft is due, so much the better.

Don't Focus Too Much on the Thesis. For now just tell yourself that it's fine if you have a **working thesis**. This can be a basic statement of the essay's main idea. Don't worry about making it perfect or eloquent or fully developed. Right now, it's just a place marker; a way to keep yourself focused on what you write, and not much more. The student writing about the first day of college in Chapter Two could have a working thesis reading something like: "My first day of college was a rite of passage that taught me a lot about myself." As the essay progresses, the student will need to go back and elaborate on what he or she means by "taught me a lot," but at this stage of the paper, the student may not yet know what the first day of college taught him or her and so should not try to force the thesis to be more developed than it can be.

Work From a Rough Outline. Some people don't like outlines because they have been taught that outlines must be formal and must not be deviated from. If that is how you've thought of outlines before, try to think of this instead as a rough or informal list of the things you plan on writing about and in what order. Referring to your outline can help keep you focused, saving you from getting off track as you work your way through the draft.

Think about Grammar, but Don't Over-Think. Avoiding errors as you write a first draft is, of course, a good idea, and if you focus more on grammar than on content in the early stages of your draft, it will be easier for you to move through the editing process. That said, you should still avoid worrying too much about *how* you're saying things in your paper and concentrate at this point simply on *what* you're saying.

If You Get Stuck, Go Back to Invention. The writing process is not a one-way street. If you find yourself running out of ideas as you draft, it may not be a case of "writer's block" but rather a case of your not having fully thought through all the issues related to your topic. You probably assumed you had done this, but when you hit a creative wall after a page and a half, that's probably a signal that more **Invention** is necessary. Spend a half hour or so with some of the techniques in Chapter Two and see if they help get you back on track.

Save Everything. Whether you compose your draft with pencil and paper or on a computer, it is essential that you save your work as it progresses. Don't throw away old drafts or parts of drafts until you are completely finished with your paper; you never know when you might reconsider getting rid of an idea and want to restore it to the draft. This is especially true once you begin typing your draft into a word processing program like Microsoft Word. Hit the "Save" button frequently so that your work is preserved in case of computer malfunctions. If you remove large sections of your draft, rather than use the "cut" or "delete" functions, it is better to cut and paste those sections into another file for safe keeping in case you change your mind later. When finished with your draft, make sure you save it to a location you can access again—such as your computer's hard drive or to a flash drive if you use different computers. This way, you can make changes to the draft along the way and won't have to re-type the paper if you have the opportunity to revise it later.

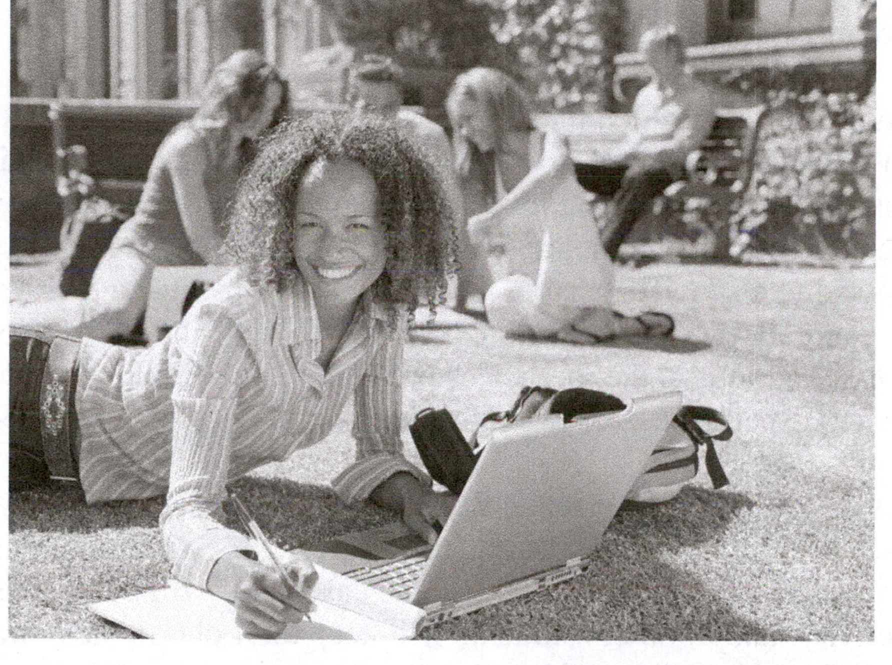

Chapter Four: Getting Feedback

Constructive Criticism

As long as you write only for yourself—in a journal or diary entry, for instance, or in a quick note to remind yourself of something you need to do—taking your audience into consideration is not something you generally concern yourself with. You know what you mean when you write for yourself. It is when you write for someone else—for an audience beyond yourself—that you need to begin concerning yourself with things like organization, word choice and grammar.

As academic writers, this becomes especially important. Most students like to think of their instructor as their primary audience in this kind of setting, but most instructors prefer that their students try to write for what is called a "general public" audience. In other words, rather than try to guess what will appeal to a specific person—your professor, for instance—you should think of your audience as a group of reasonably well-informed people who share some opinions and experiences but who are also quite diverse in terms of beliefs, specialized knowledge, etc.

As a way to help you relate to such an audience and to give you a sense of how your draft is progressing, most instructors will have students engage in some form of peer review. In some cases, this will be done as an in-class activity, and in others students will keep their classmates' drafts for a day or two and return them with peer reviews.

This can be a bit intimidating for some students who feel that they are not in a position to judge the work of their peers since they have not yet mastered the type of writing being taught in the class. You should note, however, that most instructors do not expect their students to read other students' papers as experts, but rather to give them a sense of how their audience is responding to their work. Thus, you need to focus on providing good **constructive criticism** for your peers.

To give constructive criticism, you need to point out:

- **What works well and why**
- **What still needs work and why**

This is not the same as telling the student what is right or wrong, good or bad. Instead, you are treating the draft as a work in progress and letting the student know what he or she should focus on as the paper develops. Thus, if you find yourself interested, intrigued, or amused by the whole paper or parts of it, you can let the writer know how and why the paper appealed to you. This is far more effective than writing something general like "Good job. Keep up the good work." A student receiving that sort of feedback really won't know what he or she has done well and won't know how to develop those successful elements of the essay further.

On the other hand, if you find the writing confusing, lacking in focus, uninteresting or difficult to understand, you can let the writer know where the trouble spots are (in a supportive way) and thus give your classmate a sense of what to focus on as he or she begins the revision process. Explaining the problems in the paper this way does not require you to have any specialized knowledge about grammar or to be in any way an expert. You are simply giving your classmate a sense of how and why the paper did not appeal to you.

A Starting Point

Before considering peer review any further, take the time to read the following rough draft. The draft was written in response to this assignment: "Using specific examples, write an essay in which you describe a person who had a significant impact on your life and explain what that impact was." As you read, think about the kinds of constructive criticism you would give if the student was in your peer review group.

A Mighty Heart

My Uncle Gerald was a remarkable guy. It wasn't that he did big things in his life. He really didn't. It was more the way he lived—and ultimately the way he died. I remember the first time I met him, he came up to our front door when I was about twelve—a friendly looking, gray-haired man who knew my name.

My parents let him in, and then I realized that this was the uncle I had always heard stories about as I was growing up—the uncle who had run away from home at 15, who had been in the Canadian army, who had hopped freight trains and ridden his way across Canada and the United States, and who had had multiple bypass surgery before he was forty. He stayed a few days and then was gone again. Over the next few years, he would breeze through my life this way a few more times, and every time I saw him, I couldn't get enough of his stories and his laughter. My Uncle Gerald had a great impact on me, teaching me the value of a life lived on your own terms.

One of the stories he told me that made a real impression was about when he was working in a mine in the Yukon Territory. This was during the time when he had been a teenage runaway. The mine was a few miles away from the town where the workers lived. A bus took the miners from the town to the mine, but they had to pay a fare to ride to work. If they could not afford it, they had to walk to the mine in the morning and back to town again in the evening. Every Friday was payday, and every Friday Uncle Gerald told himself he would be riding the bus on Monday. But every Friday night, there was a poker game, and every Monday he was walking to work again. Eventually, he must have learned from his mistakes and saved enough money to get out of the mine, but there was something about that story that struck me, something about the way he kept making the same mistakes over and over again.

He told me that story one morning when I was about 20 years old. He had shown up at our door a few days before after having spent the winter in La Paz, Mexico, living in a little shack on the beach. As winter was ending, he was on his way back to Canada, and his next stop would be Las Vegas. He left on a Greyhound bus that afternoon.

He died that same night, having a massive heart attack while sitting on a barstool in a Las Vegas casino. When we read the police report later, it made it sound like he had been dead before he hit the floor. His death was a total shock. Uncle Gerald's energy and his laugh had been so real when he had been at our house, and now he was gone. In retrospect, I remembered him mentioning that during the winter in La Paz, he had noticed his hands getting numb at night, which was probably a sign that the heart disease he had had as a younger man was returning. I also remembered how he had often regretted having his bypass surgery in his late thirties because he had not trusted the doctors' diagnosis. He had likely maintained that same distrust of doctors as he aged, his heart getting weaker and weaker. When my parents drove to Las Vegas to claim his body and property, they found five one-hundred dollar chips from the casino where he died, along with all his other money. He had, no doubt, had a very good night in the casino—too good, really—and his weakened heart had finally given out.

The thing was, though, that his heart in another sense was not weak. He had a great heart, a mighty heart. He was a generous, fun-loving man who had made mistakes in his life and kept on going, living life on his own terms. He had died young, only 56, and that was terrible. I wish he had lived longer; I wish I could have spent more time with him, heard more stories from him. But that was not to be. I can only hope that I can also live my life on my own terms and with as much energy and love for life as he did.

This draft is not perfect—far from it. In fact, it needs a lot of work. But it *is* a start, and from here the student writer can begin working on refining and improving the essay. Receiving feedback from fellow students will be the first step in that process.

The Good and Bad of Peer Review

As stated earlier, effective peer review takes the form of constructive criticism in which readers explain what works and why; as well as what still needs work and why. The emphasis here should be on **explaining** your response rather than simply identifying the strong or weak parts of the draft.

Here is an example of a peer review that would **not** be helpful to the writer of the paper above:

Instructions: Answer the following questions thoroughly and in complete sentences. Remember that the only worthwhile criticism is constructive criticism. Your job here is to show the writer what works well in his/her draft, what still needs work, and why you think so.

1. Does the introduction get the reader's attention? If so, how? If not, why not? What could the author do to make the introduction more interesting?

Yes, it gets my attention. Good hook.

2. Does the draft present a clear, effective thesis that directly responds to the essay assignment? In other words, does the

thesis let you know what the essay is going to be about in a clear, interesting way? How could the thesis be improved? Was it easy or difficult to find?

Yes, you have a good thesis. Can't think of how to improve it. Keep up the good work.

3. Do the body paragraphs develop and support the thesis? Are there any paragraphs that don't seem connected to the thesis? If so, explain. Are there any paragraphs that do not seem unified? If so, explain. What is the strongest paragraph and why?

Yes, they are good. They all seem unified. I liked the paragraph where you tell the story about the mine.

4. Does the draft present specific, descriptive details that show rather than tell? Where should more details be added? What is the most effective use of detail? Why?

Yes, good details. Maybe say more about how you felt. The most effective details were about the mine and how he died.

5. What is the strongest part of this draft and why? What still needs the most work and why?

Your descriptions. Everything else is good. Keep up the good work!! ☺

Again, this peer response does not provide constructive criticism, nor is it very insightful or informative. The answers are not specific or direct. And while being told to keep up the good work may be nice, the student writer who receives this encouragement would get very little sense of what should be kept and what should be deleted in his or her essay as it gets revised.

Consider this peer review of the same paper in contrast:

Instructions: Answer the following questions thoroughly and in complete sentences. Remember that the only worthwhile criticism is constructive criticism. Your job here is to show the writer what works well in his/her draft, what still needs work, and why you think so.

1. Does the introduction get the reader's attention? If so, how? If not, why not? What could the author do to make the introduction more interesting?

It gives some good details, but it's not quite as interesting as it could be. You need a stronger hook that gets the reader's attention from the start. Since you're telling his story throughout the essay, maybe start with something else that doesn't exactly have to do with your uncle. Try a quotation or a question.

2. Does the draft present a clear, effective thesis that directly responds to the essay assignment? In other words, does the thesis let you know what the essay is going to be about in a clear, interesting way? How could the thesis be improved? Was it easy or difficult to find?

The thesis gets the job done right now, but it's kind of basic. Say more about how his life impacted you. Was it just about living on his own terms? Do you really mean that, especially since he didn't live very long? Try to think more about how this affected you. The thesis was easy to find; it's just not as developed as it could be.

3. Do the body paragraphs develop and support the thesis? Are there any paragraphs that don't seem connected to the thesis? If

so, explain. Are there any paragraphs that do not seem unified? If so, explain. What is the strongest paragraph and why?

The body paragraphs do support the thesis, and are all related to your uncle. However, it's not always clear what their main idea is or how they show something about how his life affected you. The point you make toward the end about him being a good-hearted person seems almost like an afterthought. The paragraph about the mine is the strongest since it is the most vivid and tells us the most about him.

4. Does the draft present specific, descriptive details that show rather than tell? Where should more details be added? What is the most effective use of detail? Why?

You're specific in the mine paragraph and also with the details about how he died. There's not much of you in this draft, though, or enough details about what you thought and felt or even about why he made such a big impact on you. Was it just that he died so suddenly? If he hadn't died after telling you the story about the mine, would it have had the same impact on you?

5. What is the strongest part of this draft and why? What still needs the most work and why?

The strongest part is the emotional connection you feel toward your uncle and the way that comes through. It gives me a clear sense of your feelings. The essay mostly needs a stronger thesis and clearer organization since it's not always clear where you're going with the descriptions and ideas.

This response does make good use of constructive criticism. When the student reviewer reads something he or she likes, something that strikes the reviewer as effective or clear writing, he or she identifies it and explains what is effective about it. The student receiving this feedback would have a better sense of what to begin focusing on in revision.

This is the kind of feedback you should strive to provide your peers when given the chance.

The **questionnaire** style of gathering feedback (above) is typically used in classes where peer review is done as an in-class activity. In other cases, you may be asked to take your peers' papers home with you and write up a **detailed response**.

Here is an example of an effective peer review written in this method. Note that you should address the author by name, point out the general strengths and areas that need improvement and then make specific suggestions, explaining why you think something should be kept or changed. Remember to close by thanking the author for the opportunity to read his or her work.

Author: Joe Student
Reviewer: Jane Scholar

Dear Joe,
I enjoyed reading your paper. You are working with an interesting subject. So far, the draft has some good details, and you definitely give the reader a sense of how connected you felt to your uncle. As you continue, I think you're going to need to work on making the paper more focused and on doing more to explain how he was a significant person in your life.

The two strongest sections of the paper are where you tell the story about the mine and where you describe how he died. You use clear, specific details here to show the reader what happened. In other parts of the paper, you're not being as detailed as you could be.

Try to work on developing a stronger thesis. The thesis in this draft gets the job done, but it could be more fully developed.

Look at some of the points you're making in the conclusion about your uncle and his impact on you. Not all of those ideas seem supported in the paper, but they also seem pretty strong. You might want to take some of those ideas from the conclusion and use them to develop a stronger thesis. Then work on providing more support for those ideas about your uncle's significance and impact in the body of the essay.

I don't notice many problems with grammar. Some of the phrasing seems kind of casual, so you might want to work on making the essay sound more academic as you revise.

Thanks for letting me read your paper. It has given me some ideas for how to proceed on my own essay.

Once you have given and received feedback from your peers, instructor or anyone else whose opinion about writing you value, it's time to move into the revision process.

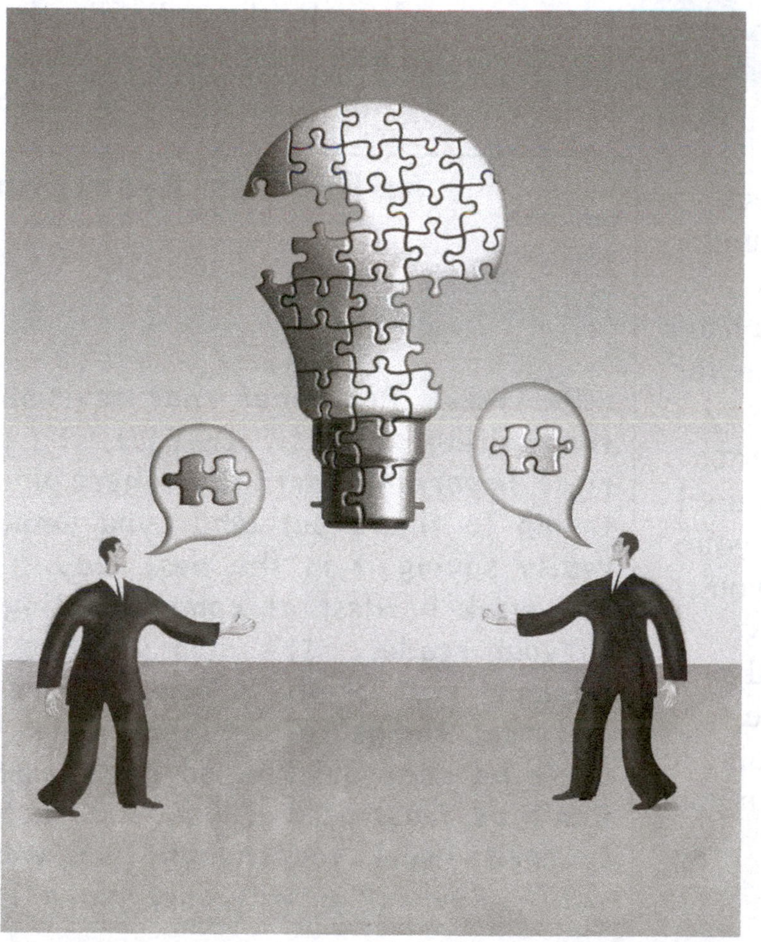

Chapter Five: Revision

Just What Is Revision, Exactly?

Many students finish the first draft of their papers and feel hopeful that they are almost finished with the whole project. In a perfect world, all they would need to do is proofread and spell check and turn the paper in for a grade.

In contrast, however, the first draft is your first attempt at working your way through your ideas. Realistically, it probably is not the best or most effective way for those ideas to be expressed. Think about your first day of college. You probably felt a bit shaky, unsure of where you were supposed to park, where your classes were, how to find the bookstore or places to eat, etc.

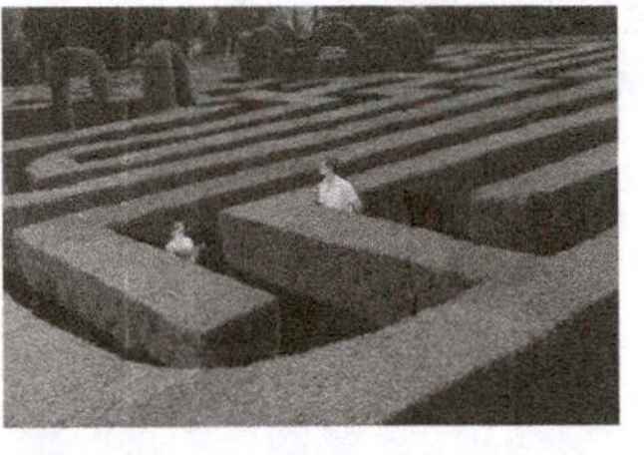

The second day was probably a bit better. You felt more confident and based your decisions on what little experience you had. By the end of the first week, you likely had a much stronger sense of where to go, when to go there, and what to do once you arrived.

The movement from rough draft to revision is similar. You had a sense of where the essay was going when you started the draft, but until you finished your conclusion, you could not have known exactly what path the paper was going to take. As with your first day of

Attitude Is Everything

Remember that revision is part of the writing process. In fact, it's probably the most important part; it's where you go from trying to figure out what you want to say to really saying it in the best way. It's where you work hardest at communicating your ideas to your reader. It's also perhaps the most difficult part of the process where you try different things to see what works best. It can't be done quickly, so don't rush yourself. Don't be frustrated if your instructor asks you to revise work you thought you were done with. Revising it will only make it better.

college, you probably took some wrong turns in the draft before getting to the final destination. Now you need to go back and work your way through the draft again—and again—refining it as you go.

When you revise, you will be engaging in four basic activities:

- Adding
- Deleting
- Rearranging
- Rephrasing

Adding. You will likely need to add details and examples to your draft. It is possible that you will need to add whole paragraphs and probably a new thesis.

Deleting. This is a more painful process for someone who has labored over a draft, but it is just as crucial to the revision process—if not more so. Just as you are adding examples, details, sentences and paragraphs, you may also need to delete examples, details, sentences and whole paragraphs that were in the first draft. Don't make the mistake of insisting on leaving material in the draft simply because you wrote it.

Rearranging. The order in which you arranged your paragraphs in the first draft may not be the best. Your thesis may focus on ideas in a certain order, but the body paragraphs may be in a different order; consider revising so the two parts of the essay match. You should also consider how the different topics are arranged in the body of the essay; are you organizing it chronologically, in order of importance, or some other method? Is it the best plan? Be open to the possibility of moving things around.

Rephrasing. It should come as no surprise that the words you chose in putting together your first draft may not be the best words with which to get your point across. They may not be the most descriptive, accurate or clear words and phrases, and you will need to spend some time looking carefully at the language in your draft as you move toward being ready to turn it in for a final grade. As you will see later in this chapter, you will be better off saving this part of the revision process for close to the end.

After receiving the type of feedback discussed in Chapter Four, you are ready to begin revising your essay, focusing on building from its strengths and eliminating its weaknesses. In the process of **adding** material to make the draft stronger and **deleting** other elements of it that don't work, you will focus on your essay's **content**. Once you are sure you have everything in the essay that it needs and have gotten rid of what it doesn't need, you can begin **rearranging** the material to put it in the best **order** possible. Finally, you will work on **rephrasing** sections of the essay, putting emphasis on the paper's **voice**.

Revising for Content

Here are some questions you should ask yourself about what's actually in your essay as you begin revising:

Is your essay sufficiently addressing all parts of the writing assignment?

Your instructor has most likely asked you to do specific things in this essay, and you need to make sure you are doing all of them. Perhaps you have been asked to use specific details, to use a certain number of examples, to analyze your examples, etc. Most instructors check to make sure you are completing all parts of the assignment.

Are your examples specific, vivid and interesting?

There is a difference between **showing** and **telling**. The examples you use will be much more effective if they are specifically detailed and thus show the reader what you mean. Examples that merely *tell* are boring. If you find yourself relying on words like "things," "people," "everyone," "someone," "a person," "you," etc., then you should replace them with specific examples. Try to use comparisons to help readers understand concepts they may not be familiar with.

Does your essay have all of its parts?

Is there a fully developed introduction with an interesting hook, some background material, and a clear thesis? Make sure you have sufficient body paragraphs with detailed examples and that the connection between the examples and the thesis is clear. Does your conclusion merely summarize, or does it leave the reader with some final ideas on the subject?

Revising for Order

Here are some things to consider regarding your essay's organization:

Do you have a clear, fully developed thesis?

If your thesis does not fit the description of a strong thesis on page 20, then going back into it and developing it more fully is one of the first things you should do. Remember that your thesis needs to identify the essay's topic and present your point of view about that topic in a clear, logical, specific way.

Is each body paragraph clearly organized and unified?

Remember that each body paragraph needs to be doing something specific in the paper and that the writer should know the purpose and function of each paragraph in his or her essay. If you don't know what a paragraph's main idea is, you can be sure that your reader won't know either. Once you know what the main idea is, check to make sure you have a topic sentence that states the main idea, and then read each paragraph carefully to be sure there is nothing in it that is off-topic or making the paragraph lack unity.

Are your ideas arranged in the most effective order?

Just because your rough draft developed topics A, B and C (in that order), you should not feel locked into that pattern of organization. Experiment and ask yourself if it might make more sense to arrange it in A, C, B order. You can arrange your ideas according to time (chronological storytelling), order of importance (most to least, least to most, etc.) or logically (having one idea develop out of the previous one). Consider your audience's needs and what they will likely need to know first, second and so on in order for your ideas to make sense.

Revising for Voice

Finally, here are some things to ask yourself about the words you've chosen:

Are the language and tone appropriate to the topic and assignment?

Make sure that your writing is more formal than the language you might use communicating with your friends or in the contents of an email or text message. Don't use slang, and don't use abbreviations like "u" for "you." Similarly, don't try to sound too formal. If you're relying on a thesaurus to put impressive-sounding words into the essay, it's probably a mistake since words you're likely unfamiliar with may not come across the right way, or they may make it seem too obvious that you're writing out of your element. Regarding tone, try to sound serious as long as the assignment does not call for humor. Remember that you are writing academic discourse, so you need to take a serious, studious tone.

Are you using the best words?

Later on, we will examine word choice more fully. For now, you need to use a good, critical eye to examine the words and phrases you have used in your essay. Consult the section on commonly confused words later in this book and read your draft carefully to avoid errors. Also, make sure that any words you're using that you are not completely sure of are, in fact, getting across the meaning you intended. This may require you to have someone else read the essay.

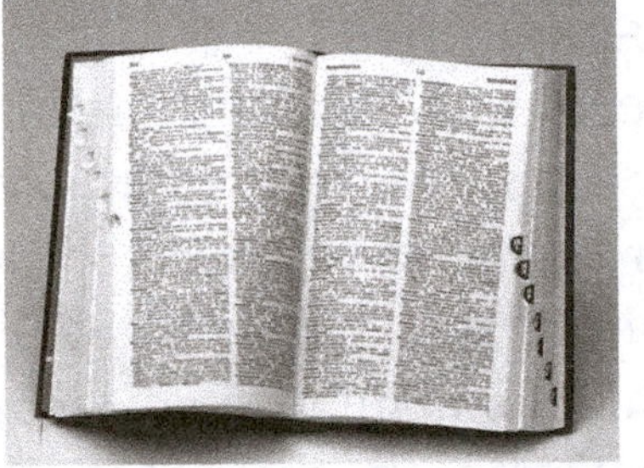

Are there any words you're repeating too much?

If you find that the same word or phrase appears multiple times in a paragraph or in several connected sentences, consider revising. You could combine ideas from several sentences into one to eliminate repetition, or you could use suitable synonyms. Also, if you find that every sentence in a paragraph starts with the same word, phrase, or type of word, try to use some variety, moving the subject to the middle of the sentence occasionally, starting with some descriptive words before using the subject, etc.

Revision at Work

Taking the advice of peers and putting a lot more thought into the subject, the student author of "A Mighty Heart" (included in Chapter Four) worked on revising the essay. Note that material has been added, deleted, rearranged and rephrased and that there has been revision of content, organization and voice. The student developed a stronger hook, a clearer thesis and a better sense of the essay's organization. More importantly, the author now has a clearer understanding of the essay's subject, and the new title reflects this.

The paragraphs below show the original draft and the changes that have been made to it. Deleted material appears with ~~the strikethrough line~~; the underlined material has been added; everything else has remained unchanged. Take a few moments to skim through this edited version to see how little of the original material has remained unchanged. The final draft without the editing marks appears after this version, and it would be a good idea to read that draft carefully, perhaps comparing it to the draft version that appeared in Chapter Four.

~~A Mighty Heart~~The Gamble

~~My Uncle Gerald was a remarkable guy. It wasn't that he did big things in his life. He really didn't. It was more the way he lived and ultimately the way he died.~~ Mark Twain once wrote that if a cat sits on a hot stove one time, it will never sit on a hot stove again—but it will also never sit on a cold stove either. In other words, cats may not be smart enough to know the difference between a hot and a cold stove, but they are at least smart enough to learn from their mistakes. Learning from one's mistakes is something not everyone seems able to do, which is something I think about when I remember my Uncle Gerald. ~~I remember t~~ I was about twelve the first time I met him ~~him, he came up to our front door when I was about twelve~~—a friendly looking, gray-haired man who came up to our front door and ~~knew my~~addressed me by name. ~~My parents let him in, and then~~ I soon realized that this was the uncle I had always heard stories about as I was growing up—the uncle who had run away from home at 15, who had ~~been~~ ended up in the Canadian army, who had hopped freight trains and ridden his way across Canada and the United States, and who had had multiple bypass surgery before he was forty. After ~~He~~ he stayed a few days, ~~and then~~ he was gone again. Over the next few years, he would breeze through my life this way a few more times, and every time I saw him, I couldn't get enough of his stories and his laughter. There was more to him than that, though. He lived and died on his own terms, and even though he seemed to love every minute of his life, he also never seemed to break himself of the habit of repeating the same mistakes. When I remember him, I find myself wishing I could live as freely as he did, but I also realize the cost was too high.~~My Uncle Gerald had a great impact on me, teaching me the value of a life lived on your own terms.~~

The last time I saw him was when he stopped by our house on his way back to Canada after having spent the winter living in a shack on the beach in La Paz, Mexico. He told me a story I will never forget. ~~One of the stories he told me that made a real impression was about when~~ During the time when he had been a teenage runaway, he ~~was~~ worked ~~ing~~ in a mine in the Yukon Territory. ~~This was during the time when he had been a teenage runaway~~. ~~The mine was a few miles away from the town where the workers lived.~~ The mine being a few miles from the town where the miners lived, they had to walk to and from work or else ride a bus. ~~A bus took the miners from the town to the mine, but they had to pay a fare to ride to work. If they could not afford it, they had to walk to the mine in the morning and back to town~~

~~again in the evening.~~ But the bus cost money, and Uncle Gerald had none. So e~~E~~very Friday when he would get paid,~~was payday, and every Friday Uncle Gerald~~ he told himself he would be riding the bus on Monday. But every Friday night, there was a poker game~~, ~~—and every Monday he was walking to ~~work~~ the mine again. ~~Eventually, he must have learned from his mistakes and save enough money to get out of the mine, but there was something about that story that struck me, something about the way he kept making the same mistakes over and over again.~~I remember how he laughed as he told this story—laughing at himself, really, and how foolish he had been. When he laughed, his whole face would crinkle up, his eyes all but disappearing amidst deep wrinkles, and he would repeat the punch line of a story through the laughter, barely able to get the words out.

He died that same night, after having left our house and taken a bus to Las Vegas. When I read the police report later, I learned that he had a massive heart attack while sitting on a barstool in a Las Vegas casino. The report made it sound like he had been dead before he hit the floor. He was only 56 years old.

~~He told me that story one morning when I was about 20 years old. He had shown up at our door a few days before after having spent the winter in La Paz, Mexico, living in a little shack on the beach. As winter was ending, he was on his way back to Canada, and his next stop would be Las Vegas. He left on a Greyhound bus that afternoon.~~

~~He died that same night, having a massive heart attack while sitting on a barstool in a Las~~

~~Vegas casino~~. ~~When we read the police report later, it made it sound like he had been dead before he hit the floor. H~~ At first, his death was a total shock. ~~Uncle Gerald's energy and his laugh had been so real when he had been at our house, and now he was gone. I~~ But in retrospect, I remembered him mentioning that during the winter in La Paz, he had noticed his hands getting numb at night, which was probably a sign that the heart disease he had had as a younger man was returning. I also remembered how he had often regretted having his bypass surgery in his late thirties because he had not trusted the doctors' diagnosis. He had likely maintained that same distrust of doctors as he aged, his heart getting weaker and weaker. When my parents drove to Las Vegas to claim his body and property, they found five one-hundred dollar chips from the casino where he died, along with all his other money. He had, no doubt, had a very good night in the casino—too good, really—and his weakened heart had finally given out.

I think now about those five chips sitting in the pocket of the same man who had kept losing at poker in a Yukon mining town forty years earlier. I don't say that he had a problem with gambling—not in the usual sense. But the same impulse he had had as a teenager—to gamble on running away from home, to risk his bus money in one Friday night poker game after another—may have been the same trait that caused him to gamble with his health, to shrug off the numb hands and to insist that the bypass scar that reached from his thigh to his chest had been there at the insistence of overzealous doctors and not as a real indicator that he had a weak heart.

The simple conclusion would be that he gambled with his health and lost, but looking at his life and death this way would be to undervalue the joy he took in every aspect of his life, the way his laughter took over with every story he told. So it may be that he knew he was gambling, knew he was on the edge, knew he could die at any time, and because he knew it, he lived every minute of his short life on his own terms. When he was playing in those poker games in the Yukon, he may have been telling himself that he was running the risk of losing his bus money, but he was also just as likely having a blast, doing things he never would have dreamed of on the farms where he grew up. If someone were to measure his life by the way it ended that night in Las Vegas, then it might look like a losing hand, a long series of mistakes that would end too soon. But I prefer to think of him during that winter in La Paz, doing what he had done for years—living simply and able to laugh at everything, even himself. It was something he had probably learned to do during those poker games in the Yukon.

In the end, he did gamble with his health, but it was not done out of foolishness or recklessness. Just as the risk of having to walk to the mines had not been enough to make him change the way he lived as a teenager, so was the risk of dying not enough to make him change as a 56-year-old. To have gone to the doctors again would have been to change the way he lived, to chain himself to a regimen of medication, diet and

<u>limitation. It would have been a kind of death for him. I wish he had lived longer; I wish I could have spent more time with him, heard more stories from him. But for him to have lived longer would have meant his living differently, and not in the same spirit that had characterized every other part of his life. And while I do not plan on gambling with my health, I can only hope that I can also live my life on my own terms and with as much energy and love for life as he did.</u>

~~The thing was, though, that his heart in another sense was not weak. He had a great heart, a mighty heart. He was a generous, fun-loving man who had made mistakes in his life and kept on going, living life on his own terms. He had died young, only 56, and that was terrible. I wish he had lived longer; I wish I could have spent more time with him, heard more stories from him. But that was not to be. I can only hope that I can also live my life on my own terms and with as much energy and love for life as he did.~~

Comparing this version with the original draft, you should be able to see that the final version is stronger and more focused. More importantly, you should also note that the process of revising the essay involved more than adding a few words or correcting any problems with grammar, spelling or word choice. Here is the final version of the essay without the deleted material:

The Gamble

Mark Twain once wrote that if a cat sits on a hot stove one time, it will never sit on a hot stove again—but it will also never sit on a cold stove either. In other words, cats may not be smart enough to know the difference between a hot and a cold stove, but they are at least smart enough to learn from their mistakes. Learning from one's mistakes is something not everyone seems able to do, which is something I think about when I remember my Uncle Gerald. I was about twelve the first time I met him—a friendly looking, gray-haired man who came up to our front door and addressed me by name. I soon realized that this was the uncle I had always heard stories about as I was growing up—the uncle who had run away from home at 15, who had ended up in the Canadian army, who had hopped freight trains and ridden his way across Canada and the United States, and who had had multiple bypass surgery before he was forty. After he stayed a few days, he was gone again. Over the next few years, he would breeze through my life this way a few more times, and every time I saw him, I couldn't get enough of his stories and his laughter. There was more to him than that, though. He lived and died on his own terms, and even though he seemed to love every minute of his life, he also never seemed to break himself of the habit of repeating the same mistakes. When I remember him, I find myself wishing I could live as freely as he did, but I also realize the cost was too high.

The last time I saw him was when he stopped by our house on his way back to Canada after having spent the winter living in a shack on the beach in La Paz, Mexico. He told me a story I will never forget. During the time when he had been a teenage runaway, he worked in a mine in the Yukon Territory. The mine being a few miles from the town where the miners lived, they had to walk to and from work or else ride a bus. But the bus cost money, and Uncle Gerald had none. So every Friday when he would get paid, he told himself he would be riding the bus on Monday. But every Friday night, there was a poker game—and every Monday he was walking to the mine again. I remember how he laughed as he told this story—laughing at himself, really, and how foolish he had been. When he laughed, his whole face would crinkle up, his eyes all but disappearing amidst deep wrinkles, and he would repeat the punch line of a story through the laughter, barely able to get the words out.

He died that same night, after having left our house and taken a bus to Las Vegas. When I read the police report later, I learned that he had a massive heart attack while sitting on a barstool in a Las Vegas casino. The report made it sound like he had been dead before he hit the floor. He was only 56 years old.

At first, his death was a total shock. But in retrospect, I remembered him mentioning that during the winter in La Paz, he had noticed his hands getting numb at night, which was probably a sign that the heart disease he had had as a younger man was returning. I also remembered how he had often regretted having his bypass surgery in his late thirties because he had not trusted the doctors' diagnosis. He had likely maintained that same distrust of doctors as he aged, his heart getting weaker and weaker. When my parents drove to Las Vegas to claim his body and property, they found five one-hundred dollar chips from the casino where he died, along with all his other money. He had, no doubt, had a very good night in the casino—too good, really—and his weakened heart had finally given out.

I think now about those five chips sitting in the pocket of the same man who had kept losing at poker in a Yukon mining town forty years earlier. I don't say that he had a problem with gambling—not in the usual sense. But the same impulse he had had as a teenager—to gamble on running away from home, to risk his bus money in one Friday night poker game after another—may have been the same trait that caused him to gamble with his health, to shrug off the numb hands and to insist that the bypass scar that reached from his thigh to his chest had been there at the insistence of overzealous doctors and not as a real indicator that he had a weak heart.

The simple conclusion would be that he gambled with his health and lost, but looking at his life and death this way would be to undervalue the joy he took in every aspect of his life, the way his laughter took over with every story he told. So it may be that he *knew* he was gambling, knew he was on the edge, knew he could die at any time, and because he knew it, he lived every minute of his short life on his own terms. When he was playing in those poker games in the Yukon, he may have been telling himself that he was running the risk of losing his bus money, but he was also just as likely having a blast, doing things he never would have dreamed of on the farms where he grew up. If someone were to measure his life by the way it ended that night in Las Vegas,

> then it might look like a losing hand, a long series of mistakes that would end too soon. But I prefer to think of him during that winter in La Paz, doing what he had done for years—living simply and able to laugh at everything, even himself. It was something he had probably learned to do during those poker games in the Yukon.
>
> In the end, he did gamble with his health, but it was not done out of foolishness or recklessness. Just as the risk of having to walk to the mines had not been enough to make him change the way he lived as a teenager, so was the risk of dying not enough to make him change as a 56-year-old. To have gone to the doctors again would have been to change the way he lived, to chain himself to a regimen of medication, diet and limitation. It would have been a kind of death for him. I wish he had lived longer; I wish I could have spent more time with him, heard more stories from him. But for him to have lived longer would have meant his living differently, and not in the same spirit that had characterized every other part of his life. And while I do not plan on gambling with my health, I can only hope that I can also live my life on my own terms and with as much energy and love for life as he did.

To arrive at this final draft, the author had to re-think the material in the first draft, decide on what the essay's main idea really ought to be, and then radically revise the draft by cutting and moving material as well as adding more.

It takes some time to revise effectively and to let the process work for you. If you try to do all your revising in one session, it will probably not be as effective as it will be if you give yourself plenty of time.

Revision Strategies

Here are some strategies to consider as you revise your work:

Start with the Big Things: If peer review or your instructor's feedback has revealed that there is some part of the assignment your draft is missing, make sure you focus on that first. For example, if the writing assignment asked you to give specific examples and explain their significance, it is possible that you concentrated on using examples but forgot to explain them, making the connections between the examples and your thesis unclear. On the other hand, you may not have included a conclusion in your draft, or the rough draft may be lacking a thesis. In any case, if you find that anything is missing in your draft, make sure you include it before continuing. Failing to complete part of the assignment can result in the whole paper receiving a non-passing score.

Look Carefully at Your Conclusion: Oftentimes, when you start a rough draft, you will know what you want to write about, but you may not have a clear idea of what you want to say about your subject. As a result, the thesis in a rough draft may not be as fully developed as it should be since you wrote the thesis when you were just starting to explore the ideas in your paper. However, when you write the conclusion in a rough draft, you have a much better sense of what you want to say about your subject, and it frequently works out that there will be a sentence or two in your conclusion that could work better as a new thesis, perhaps with some minor changes. Move the new thesis into your introduction, and then revise the conclusion again.

If You're Stuck for Ideas, Go Back to Invention: As stated earlier, the writing process does not work like a one-way street. If you still have difficulty developing your main idea or connecting all the parts of your draft, go back to one of the invention strategies explained in Chapter Two. Incorporate new ideas into your draft as you start revising.

Work on One Thing at a Time: Rather than try to fix everything at once, give yourself specific tasks. First, revise for **content**, focusing on getting all the parts of your draft sufficiently developed. Next, work on **organization**, experimenting with the order of ideas in the whole essay and in individual paragraphs; make sure each paragraph has a solid topic sentence and that all paragraphs are clearly unified and relate easily to the thesis. Finally, focus on **voice**, examining word choice and phrasing. Try reading your draft out loud or have someone else read it to you, so you can see if there are any awkward phrases or unnecessary repetition.

Once you have ironed out any issues with content, organization, and voice in your essay, it's time to move on to the final phase in the process—editing and proofreading.

Revision at a Glance

- ✓ **Time**—You can't revise well if you don't give yourself plenty of time. Don't save revision until the night before an assignment is due.
- ✓ **Start with the big things** and work down to the smaller things.
- ✓ If your **thesis** needs help, look at your conclusion for ideas.
- ✓ Revision involves:
  - ✓ Adding
  - ✓ Deleting
  - ✓ Rearranging
  - ✓ Rephrasing

- ✓ Start with:
  - ✓ Content
    - ✓ Are all **parts of the prompt** being addressed?
    - ✓ Are your examples **interesting** and **specific**?
    - ✓ Do you have **introduction**, **thesis**, **body paragraphs** and **conclusion**?
  - ✓ Order
    - ✓ Do you have a clear, fully developed **thesis**?
    - ✓ Are your body paragraphs clearly **organized** and **unified**?
    - ✓ Are ideas arranged in the most **effective sequence**?
  - ✓ Voice
    - ✓ Are you using appropriate **tone** and **language**?
    - ✓ Are you using **words that mean what you think** they do?
    - ✓ Have you **avoided repetition** as much as possible?

Chapter Six: Editing and Preparing the Final Draft

Editing Your Work

Most student writers have had the experience of having a graded paper returned to them and feeling surprised at how many mistakes have been marked. Usually, these are mistakes that the writer would have caught if he or she had taken more time proofreading and editing. A student may know the difference between *to, too,* and *two*, but while engaged in the writing process, there is sometimes a breakdown between the student's brain, eyes and hands, and the wrong word gets used. Then if the student does not carefully read what has been written, the mistake goes unnoticed.

Your finished product will be stronger, and your grades will likely improve if you take the time to proofread and edit your essay once you have completed the revision process to your satisfaction. Here is where you need to concern yourself with the rules of grammar as well as conventional spelling and punctuation. Getting your essay ready to turn in for a final grade is not something you should rush. Take your time and consider the following:

Start with Your Weaknesses. If you know a particular aspect of grammar has been a trouble spot for you in the past, make sure you focus on that now. Maybe you've been told that spelling is an issue for you or that you have to watch out for sentence fragments. Perhaps a previous paper earned a low score because of problems with subject-verb agreement or shifts in verb tense. Regardless of the problem, if you know you have a particular weakness, it is in your best interest to read through the draft several times looking for that specific issue. Review the rules associated with your trouble spots and do your best to avoid the errors you may have made in the past. If you don't know your weaknesses, then do your best to catch errors and try to take note of your trouble spots as you move from essay to essay.

Work from a Hard Copy. When most students read material on a computer screen, they tend to skip over many of their errors. Perhaps this is because we are used to reading quickly when looking at computers. In any case, you will likely find more of your errors if you print a copy of your paper and sit down with it, going over it with a pen in your hand and marking anything that needs to be fixed. Go back into your computer file when you are finished and input the corrections. It will probably be a good idea to do this more than once.

Read Your Essay Aloud. When we read silently, we usually read much faster than we would be able to if we read out loud. Forcing your mouth to form the words slows you down, and when you slow down, you are more likely to find simple mistakes you would have otherwise missed. For instance, you may know the difference between "their" and "there," but if you are reading quickly, you may not notice that you accidentally used the wrong one in your essay. Reading out loud can also help you find places where your phrasing is a bit awkward. If you find yourself having to stop and read a phrase or sentence more than once to be able to get the meaning out of it, your reader will likely have the same problem. Mark it and revise it.

Have Someone You Trust Read Your Essay to You. This is a variation on reading your own essay out loud. If you trust someone who reads well to read your essay to you, it can also help you notice places where the language does not sound quite right. Unless your reader is also apt to catch grammar or spelling errors, doing this won't help with those kinds of problems, but it can help you catch some awkward or unclear phrases.

Read Your Essay Backwards. This may sound strange, but reading an essay backwards—starting with the final sentence, then the one before it, and the one before that one—will force you to see every sentence individually. By the time you have reached this stage in the writing process, you probably know what to expect as you read your essay from beginning to end, and if you are reading with the expectation of seeing something specific in your sentence, it is likely that you will see what you want to see. Again, you may know the difference between "their" and "there," but reading too quickly will lead to your missing those mistakes. If you read bottom to top, you are less likely to know what's coming next and will therefore see each sentence on its own. Any errors in them will probably stand out to you.

Use Your Spell Check. Most professors would not consider this cheating. Your word processor has a spell check feature. Use it. Don't, however, rely solely on it. If "their" and "there" are spelled correctly but used incorrectly, your spell checker won't help. Some spell checking software has an "autocorrect" feature that will go through a text and make the corrections for you. This is NOT recommended, as you may end up with an essay about the "Untied States" because your smart spell checker thought that was what you meant.

Preparing the Final Draft

Once you have proofread and edited to your satisfaction, it's time to prepare the final draft for grading. Most English courses expect final drafts to be in MLA format.

- In MLA, everything in the essay is double-spaced.
- In the header, put your last name and the page number in the top right corner.
- On the first page, list your name, your instructor's name, the course and the date on the first four lines. This information does not appear on the following pages. Don't put this information in the header; if you do, it will appear on every page.
- Center your title on the next line. Your title should be in the same font and size as the rest of the paper. Don't use **boldface**, <u>underlining</u>, ALL CAPS, "quotation marks" or anything else out of the ordinary for your title.
- Begin the first line of your essay on the next line with no extra spaces after the title.
- Use 1-inch margins all around.
- Staple the pages of your paper.

On the following page is an example of how your first page should look.

Last Name 1

Your Name

Instructor

Course

Date

Your Title Goes Here

Start your essay here. Note that there is nothing fancy about your title: no italics, underlining, all capital letters, quotation marks, etc. You also don't need to hit "Enter" extra times before or after the title to put more white space around it.

Indent the first line of each paragraph 5 spaces, and don't add extra spaces between paragraphs. Everything in your paper must be double-spaced, including the heading at the top of page one. Use 1-inch margins on all four sides of the page. Most word processors have this set as the default, but if yours has a different setting, you will need to change it.

A few final pointers:

- Proofread your draft one more time once you have printed the final copy. If you notice errors, correct them.
- Make sure your printer has plenty of ink and that the essay is legible on all pages, not just the first page.
- Make sure all pages are there and in the correct order.

Chapter Seven: Developing an Essay That Tells a Story

As an academic writer, you will encounter a variety of writing tasks and situations. In your major courses, there will likely be specific expectations and conventions that you should follow. You will do well to inquire of your instructors in those courses the specific things that are expected of you regarding tone, content, organization, etc.

Similarly, as you advance into other composition courses, you can expect that your instructor will have specific requirements based on the things discussed earlier in this guide. One other requirement, however, is that your essay be developed in specific ways. Typically, assignments fall into a few categories:

- Essays that tell a story
- Essays that explain
- Essays that argue

In this chapter, we will focus on essays that tell a story, and the other methods of development will be discussed later. There may be other writing situations you will encounter as you develop as an academic writer, but your instructors should give you specific guidelines and expectations. Make sure you follow the guidelines and meet all of the requirements and expectations.

Essays That Tell a Story

When asked to write an essay that tells a story, students are being asked to **narrate**. Usually, a **remembered event** essay will ask students to provide the details of an event and to explain something about the importance of that event. Occasionally, you may be asked to write an essay that is purely narrative, but this is unusual in academic writing.

When writing this type of essay, you need to focus on **showing** rather than telling, using **specific examples** to show your reader what you mean. To do this, try to:

- Use **sensory details**—because your reader did not share this experience with you, use details that show the reader what things sounded like, how they looked, what color things were, how things smelled, etc.
- Use **specific details**—don't assume the reader knows what you mean; slow down and help the reader get a sense of what happened.
- Use **proper names** when possible—instead of *car*, say *Lexus*; instead of vague terms like *people* or *things*, use people's names or say what the specific things were.
- Use **comparisons**—use similes and metaphors to give your reader a clearer sense of what things looked, sounded or felt like.
- Use **dialogue** when possible—if a person in your story said something, include the actual words (My father said, "Congratulations! Now

Getting Poetic

One thing that can really bring life to your descriptions is the addition of metaphors and similes—two uses of language more often associated with poetry. When you write a description, you are trying to help your reader understand something that may be unfamiliar. So you use metaphors and similes to make connections between the familiar and the unfamiliar to help the reader see your point.

Consider these lines from poet Carl Sandburg:
"The fog comes/on little cat feet./It sits looking/over harbor and city/on silent haunches/and then moves on."

Here, something the reader may not be able to grasp (this particular fog) is compared with something that can be imagined by most readers (a cat).

Now look at this example from Samuel Taylor Coleridge:
"Idle as a painted ship upon a painted ocean"

In this example, the unfamiliar thing (being idle) is described as being *similar* to a painted ship on a painted ocean, a situation where there can be no movement at all.

When you write descriptions, try to include metaphors and similes to help your reader understand your point.

> **A metaphor is a comparison in which one thing is basically described as being the same as something else—as with the fog and the cat in the example above.**
>
> **A simile, on the other hand, is a comparison in which one thing is described as being similar to something else, and the comparison usually includes the words *like* or *as*—as with the ship example.**

you're an adult.") instead of reported speech (My father congratulated me and told me I was an adult.).

Here is an example of a paragraph that tells rather than shows:

> I was in a really bad car accident a while ago. It totaled my car, and I was shaken up quite a bit. The whole thing was pretty scary, but I guess I was lucky it wasn't worse.

Someone reading this paragraph likely has a difficult time knowing exactly what happened in this accident. Vague phrases like "really bad," "a while ago," "quite a bit" and "pretty scary" fail to give the reader a sense of how bad the accident was, when it happened, what type of accident it was, etc. As a result, everyone who reads this paragraph probably pictures a different accident, which is not a mark of effective writing. Instead, effective writing conveys the message that the writer intends to convey, using specific details to give the reader a clear picture of what the author wants the reader to see and understand. Compare the paragraph above with this one:

> Last May, I was in a serious car accident one morning on my way to work. I was driving my wife's little red Subaru, and as I went through an intersection a woman driving a big Chevy van ran her red light, slamming into the driver's side of my car. The impact was thunderous, making my ears ring and sending the car spinning in a circle across the street. I remember saying, "Oh my God" even though I hadn't been to church in years. Once the car stopped, I was disoriented, partially because my glasses had been knocked off in the impact and also because the whole interior was filled with a smoky powder from the air bags igniting. It smelled like the Fourth of July after the fireworks are all finished. After a few seconds, I gathered myself together, realized what had happened and tried to open the door, but it had been hit so hard that it was pushed in about eight inches and wouldn't budge, so I had to climb out the passenger side. I had been hit in the face extremely hard by the air bag, and my back and rib cage were already starting to ache from the impact. The car was history with its whole driver's side caved in and the front wheel twisted sickeningly so it didn't even touch the ground. Even so, I was able to walk away from it and still feel lucky that it wasn't worse.

This paragraph **shows** what happened, rather than telling the reader what happened. It uses **sensory details** (showing how the crash sounded and smelled), **specific details** (the type of accident, the sequence of events, the damage done to the car), **proper names** (Subaru, Chevy), **comparisons** (comparing the smell of the ignited airbag to the smell of fireworks) and a brief bit of **dialogue** (what the writer said at the moment of impact).

Your Turn

Choose one of the following brief paragraphs and expand it so that it shows rather than tells. The new paragraph should be 8-10 sentences long. Remember that your new paragraph should use **sensory details**, **specific details**, **proper names**, **comparisons**, and **dialogue** (if appropriate).

1. We worked a long time and finally got the job done. When we were finished, my boss told us that we had made him proud.
2. The party started early and lasted late. It got a bit crazy, and when it was over the back yard was a mess.
3. When I saw the car, I knew it had to be mine. It was everything I had been looking for, and though it needed some work, I just couldn't pass it by.
4. I had never been angrier. She had insulted me for the last time.
5. The stadium was full, and I looked for my family in the stands. I knew they couldn't tell where I was among all the other graduates.

In **organizing** a remembered event essay, you should use **chronological order**, telling the story in the order of what occurred. Don't use flashbacks unless you feel very strongly about doing so, as this can be confusing to the reader unless the flashback is handled expertly. Remember that you are likely telling this story to make a **point** about something, perhaps explaining how this event was meaningful or significant to you, so your thesis will probably need to express those ideas rather than just letting the reader know what event is going to be described. Following the introduction, go into the story, remembering to be as detailed as possible.

The **thesis** in a remembered event essay needs to follow the thesis guidelines listed in Chapter Three. Using specific language, it needs to identify the topic and state the writer's point of view on the topic, presenting it as an idea that is arguable or in need of explanation. In most cases, the thesis in this type of essay will not be arguable but rather will be in need of explanation. If you are writing about something from your childhood and the way it impacted you, you probably won't need to argue that it happened or that it meant something to you. Rather, if you have chosen an interesting enough topic, it will be one that your reader likely has questions about, and the point of view you are taking on this topic will need to be explained.

Here is a **working thesis** for a remembered event essay:

> Running a marathon changed my life.

This thesis identifies the topic (a marathon) and the writer's point of view (it changed the writer's life). While a reader may wonder how and why the marathon made this change, the thesis does not yet say enough about this change, nor does it present the thesis in an interesting enough way. Revising this thesis as the essay progresses, the student could develop it this way:

> Running my first marathon would be a life-changing experience, showing me not only the strength I had within myself but also the strength to be gained from finishing something I started.

The thesis now presents the topic and the point of view as something in need of further explanation; the reader now has a sense of what type of change the writer experienced. The marathon was not just a physical challenge but a personal one as well, and the author's sense of self was part of what changed.

The above thesis is part of the following paper written by college student Scott Brandes. It is in response to an assignment to describe a rite of passage the student has been through and to explain the significance of the event.

Running to Find Myself

I was thinking, "What have I got myself into?" It was a cool January morning in the Arizona desert and I was about to run my first marathon. While three semi famous pop-singers sang the national anthem, I looked around at my fellow participants. Some wore brightly colored uniforms and tiny running shorts, while others looked like they had just picked a t-shirt out of their closet that morning and decided this would be a good day for a run. Most of us were going through some sort of pre-race stretching ritual. There were thousands of people waiting to run, but I could not help but think that none of them had a past like I did. I was starting to realize this wasn't just going to be a 26.2-mile run. Running my first marathon would be a life-changing experience, showing me not only the strength I had within myself but also the strength to be gained from finishing something I started.

All my life I had been an underachiever. I drank heavily, used drugs, and was a heavy smoker. I used to sit on the barstool and talk about things I used to do and things I was going to do, but I never did anything other than order another beer. Fortunately, I had eventually changed my life, and running a marathon confirmed it.

It had all started months earlier when I responded to a piece of junk mail that invited me to come to an information meeting given by an organization called Team In Training. They are a fundraising branch of the Leukemia and Lymphoma society. I thought I might possibly attempt a half-marathon, but when I told that to one of the coaches she looked me up and down and said that she trained middle aged women to run full marathons. She was cute and my ego was challenged, so I said, "Well, I guess I'll be running the full then." After months of grueling, sometimes torturous training, my teammates and I found ourselves in Phoenix ready to run the P.F. Chang's Rock n Roll marathon.

After the national anthem, the governor of Arizona shot off the starter's pistol, and the wheel chair racers took off with us close behind. It was good to get moving. I was starting to feel like I was going to jump out of my skin. We were still tightly bunched together as we ran. It was like cattle being herded. There was a lot of bumping and jostling going on. People were darting in and out wherever they saw an opening. After a while we separated a little bit, and I finally got into my groove. It was still early in the morning, and the streets of Phoenix were empty except for us marathoners and a few tired looking spectators.

I was sure they were family and friends. The only sounds I could hear were thousands of footsteps echoing off of the skyscraper walls.

The longer we ran, the more spectators came out to see us. There were organized cheering sections where people dressed in wild pirate or jungle themed costumes. There were people known as stunt runners running the race as well. I saw a running Elvis, a juggler, and a guy sponsored by Jamba Juice running in a banana suit. The wealthy people of Scottsdale were having big parties on their front lawns. They were drinking Bloody Marys and eating breakfast as we ran by. An older gentleman offered us a mimosa when we got to his house.

The mile markers seemed to come up pretty quickly at the start of the race, but as the day wore on they took longer to get to even though my pace had not changed. The mental aspect of the race was becoming nearly as tough as the physical. At mile 16 I felt tired but strong as I flew by the 3:30 pace group.

I was falsely starting to think this was not going to be as bad as I thought it was. At about mile 18 the pain really started to set in. Up until that point it felt sort of manageable, but then I developed a slow burn in my legs that would not stop. With each step it felt like my quads were on fire. My legs were as heavy as tree trunks. The 3:30 pace team came running by me and soon after that the juggler passed me up. I understood what people meant by running a smart, evenly paced race. I was using all the effort I had. I noticed a guy running next to me and tried to figure out how he was running so slow and managing to keep up with me. At mile 24 I wanted to quit. My head was starting to mess with me. I was saying to myself, "What are you doing this for; you should just stop." The pain was nearly unbearable. It was like I was putting myself through a self-inflicted torture. I did not think I could go on.

But at mile 25 something happened. I have never been a religious person, but I had a spiritual moment. All my life I had felt like I was all alone—that I couldn't count on anyone but myself if I wanted to achieve something. I had always been paralyzed by a fear of failure. Instead of having the courage to attempt something I was unfamiliar with, I would mock people who actually had the guts to give new things a shot. I had an inferiority complex covered up by a superiority complex, and that is a confusing way to live. The marathon was the first thing I tried that really had the chance to end in failure.

Now, I was finally going to finish something I started. A wave of emotion swept over me that brought a lump to my throat. It gave me the jump-start I needed. When I approached the finish line, I saw my parents and sisters there cheering me on. I had put my mom through hell, and the look of joy on her face was priceless. As I crossed through the finish line, I barely had the energy to hold my arms up and smile for the camera. When I finally stopped, my legs felt like jelly. I did not think I could walk another step. I heard my name being called and turned to see a bunch of my friends running towards me. They had decided to fly out to Arizona and surprise me. It was a gesture that I will never forget, and once again I realized how fortunate I was.

Bob Marley once sang, "emancipate yourself from mental slavery, none but ourselves can free our minds." I truly understand those words now. I had been a prisoner of my own mind for many years and now I feel free. The race was like my own personal underground railroad. It started the wheels rolling on something that excites me daily as I watch my life unfold. My sense of self worth had never been higher. I was one of the lucky people who were given a second chance at life, and completing this race made me feel that if I put my mind to something I would be able to accomplish it, or at least walk away from any endeavor knowing that I gave it my best effort. I will be eternally grateful that I decided to respond to that piece of "junk" mail.

Notice the use of specific details that show what the writer experienced and how he explains in the final paragraph the ways his experiences meant something to him. Readers get a clear sense of what the writer experienced, what his background was, what things looked and felt like, what thoughts were going through his head. Since it is likely that few readers have had the experience of running a marathon, the author needs to give his readers a clear understanding of his experiences and their significance, and he achieves this through the use of specific examples, sensory details, dialogue, and figurative language. The essay is also clearly organized with a sound thesis and strong paragraphs.

Chapter Eight: Developing an Essay That Explains

When writing an essay that explains a concept or an idea, you need to use some of the same strategies used in writing a narrative, or story-telling essay. Like narratives, writing that explains (also called **expository writing)** will be much stronger if the essay uses **specific examples** and **explains their significance** or meaning.

There are some differences, of course. You will likely need a more fully developed thesis than what you might have used in a narrative essay. You will also have more choices for organizing your essay than you would have had in telling a story. Depending on the assignment you are responding to, you could use chronological order, but it is more likely that you will use some **logical** or **emphatic** order (that is, order of importance).

It is also important that you have a clear point in mind when putting together your essay. This should not be a report in which you present the facts about your subject. Rather, you need a point of view, an **opinion** on the significance or value or meaning of the subject you are writing about. Arriving at such a point of view will probably require you to do some thoughtful invention before you begin drafting and revising. Keep focused on your point of view and on explaining it for a reader who either is unfamiliar with the thing you're explaining or does not see its meaning, value or importance in the same way you do. It is your job in such an assignment to help the reader see why you hold the opinion that you do regarding your subject.

It's a bit of a cliché, but one piece of advice writers always receive is that they should "write what they know." Half the battle in writing a solid expository essay comes from choosing a suitable topic, one that you find interesting, can develop an opinion on, and can make interesting and compelling for your reader. This may be challenging depending on the assignment your instructor gives you, but whenever you can, try to write on a topic you have strong feelings about.

Here, then is a quick breakdown of the writing process specifically for expository essays:

- ✓ ***Unless your instructor has given you very specific guidelines on what you must write about, the first step is to choose your topic. Do this by using the Invention strategies from Chapter Two. If no clear topic emerges at first, keep trying, using different Invention techniques until something emerges.***
- ✓ ***Once you have arrived at a topic, try some more focused Invention techniques on the topic itself. Try to write, list, or cluster everything you can think of regarding the topic, including questions that might be asked by a reader who doesn't know the subject as well as you do. Don't settle for the first things that come to mind. Push yourself to write a thorough list, even including things you think won't make it into the essay itself. It's better to be over-prepared rather than under-prepared.***
- ✓ ***Now it's time to come up with a working thesis. Remember that your thesis needs to express some sort of an opinion on the topic. If your instructor is asking for something specific (like a value judgment on the topic, for instance), then make sure your thesis meets the requirements. Keep in mind that this is just a working thesis; it will likely develop and change as the essay progresses.*** 
- ✓ ***Write out some questions that you think a reader might have after looking at your thesis. Try to group the questions logically and use them to help you decide the types of things your body paragraphs should address.***
- ✓ ***Make a list of examples that will help a reader understand your topic as well as the position you're taking on that topic.***
- ✓ ***Using your groups of questions and examples, put together a rough outline for the essay. Ask yourself how it should be organized, taking into consideration which topics or examples might be more or less interesting to a reader and which ones should be discussed before others for purposes of clarity.***
- ✓ ***Work on a good hook for your introduction and a bit of background before including your thesis.***
- ✓ ***Develop your examples around the same principles you used in writing a narrative essay—solid, detailed examples and brief explanations of them so the reader sees the point you're trying to make.***
- ✓ ***When you have finished your draft, get some feedback from peers and/or your instructor, and then follow the steps outlined in the chapter on Revision.***

Here is an essay written by student Scott Brandes in response to an assignment to explain the value of some aspect of popular culture:

Change the Channel

Angry drunken midgets, strippers, porn stars, and dirty jokes—the F.C.C. and the religious right would tell people this is a recipe for the downfall of western civilization. Others call it a typical morning on the Howard Stern show. This program has not only become the most influential radio program in history, but Howard Stern's ability to speak candidly about taboo subjects has opened up a dialogue that can not be found in other mainstream media outlets. Because Howard and the crew discuss these topics, the show has become a leader in the fight for free speech.

Someone listening to Howard's show would know that all Howard ever wanted when he was a kid was to be the host of a morning radio program. In the early 60's when he was growing up, the only people Howard ever heard on the radio were fast-talking DJs over-hyping records between spins. When F.M. radio started to get popular, the style of the radio announcer changed to a low key, counter-culture, stoner dude, but they still didn't have anything interesting to say. People would not honestly talk about what was going on in their lives. The only people who talked on the radio for any amount of time were newscasters and commentators who never strayed very far from politics and the people who were in the political world.

Then Howard came on the scene and tried to change all that. When he was a teenager, Howard was consumed by sex, as most adolescent boys are. He knew it would be funny to talk about peoples' sexual habits. There were comedians like Richard Pryor and George Carlin talking about real life from the stage, but no one was being real on the radio. There were two main topics when people talked about sex. It was considered dirty, something that should be left behind closed doors, or it was characterized as a loving, emotional bond between a man and a woman in a dark room filled with candles, incense, and flowers. While that may be a wonderful ideal, the truth is that sex can be funny and provocative. Howard came on the airways and spoke honestly about the private parts of his life when nobody else even considered it. He spoke of how awkward he felt growing up because he was not a good athlete and did not have good social skills. He admitted to being the tall, skinny, geeky kid, who got stoned and sat in the back of the classroom trying not to get noticed. But mostly he talked about the difficulties he had trying to get girls to sleep with him. He brought the male locker room talk to the public airwaves.

Advertisers have known for years that sex sells, but the sexual imagery was usually broadcast in a subliminal manner. Budweiser didn't come out and say that if you drank their beer you would get good-looking women, but they let people believe that if they drank Bud they would spend most of their day playing beach volleyball with swimsuit models. Howard was one of the first people to honestly speak up about what men really go through when it comes to the opposite sex. He talked about begging girls all night for sex and being rejected time and time again, and guys laughed because we had all been through that hell before. He spoke of feeling sexually inadequate, and we gave a little sigh of relief because most of us had those feelings at times, but nobody openly talked about them.

The Howard Stern Show has brought many taboo subjects into the forefront. Like *All In The Family* and *Blazing Saddles* before him, Howard has been able to bring up the subject of race in a humorous way.

People often characterize Howard as a racist, but if they really listened to the show they would realize he is using satire to prove a point. He often talks about growing up in an all black community, and being beaten up and getting his pants stolen because he was a white kid. These stories are not told with racist undertones; they are just funny moments from his past. When Howard and the crew put on an old time Amos and Andy voice while talking about O.J. Simpson, it is so over the top that someone would have to be clueless to take it for anything more than a joke.

The show has been criticized over the years for having on Daniel Carver of the K.K.K. Carver spouts off hateful rhetoric, and if people were told about his appearances without actually listening to them, they might think Howard was promoting the K.K.K. In reality nothing could be further from the truth. The Stern show is not agreeing with Carver; they are laughing at him. Carver is an uneducated, simple-minded fool from the backwoods of Georgia. When he talks about his hatred of all races, even most white people, it puts a face to the K.K.K., and people are made to realize that under that white sheet is a stupid man. Howard and the crew are well aware of this, and that is why they put him on. Some people would say it is in bad taste to put on a member of the K.K.K., but in doing so the Stern show takes one of the most feared organizations this country has ever known and shows that in the present day they are nothing more than a bunch of scared little men who should be belittled for their vile, hate filled views. This is able to happen because Howard is not afraid to make fun of a subject that most people do not want to go near.

Today people can see the influence of this kind of frank talk on TV from daytime talk shows like *Oprah*, network sitcoms, and especially reality television. The famous episode of *Seinfeld* where they held a contest on who could go the longest without masturbating would never have been on TV without Howard bringing that topic out in the open first. The infuriating thing is while shows like *Oprah* and *Seinfeld* receive critical approval and are widely accepted by the media, Howard is portrayed as the devil incarnate. Once when an F.C.C commissioner was questioned about why the F.C.C fined Howard for talking about a specific sexual act some gay men perform, but didn't fine Oprah for talking about exactly the same thing on her show, the commissioner answered that Oprah was a beloved figure. There should be no prejudice when it comes to the first amendment. Either we have free speech or we don't. What might be offensive to one person could be funny to another.

We live on a planet with many different cultures and customs. The differences between them can often times be humorous. We have come to a point in history where political correctness runs rampant, and even worse than that we have religious leaders who think that their interpretation of the Bible is more important than our Bill of Rights. Howard has helped many people see that we should not take ourselves so seriously. There is no topic that should not be lampooned just because someone finds it offensive. We should rejoice in the fact that we are allowed to speak about any topic we want. We should never sit idly by when our government tries to strip people of their basic rights. We slowly lose our rights when we let congress try to silence Howard Stern, or other entertainers, simply because some people are uncomfortable with how those artists choose to express themselves. If someone hates the Howard Stern show and is worried about losing his or her moral compass when hearing it, then he or she should try something crazy.

Change the channel!

This student has a clear focus—the value of the Howard Stern show—and presents specific examples of the content of the show, the humor Stern uses, and the way the show fits into other areas of popular culture, both past and present. The essay is also clearly organized, starting with a good, general introduction and following it with body paragraphs that develop the thesis. The first body paragraphs use **chronological** organization, which is then followed by paragraphs that are organized **emphatically**—moving from the less important issues of Stern's satirical handling of sex and race to the more serious (for the writer) issue of freedom of speech and the ways Stern's show points out the current trends in how free speech is handled within the media and by the government.

Furthermore, in writing an expository essay, students have several strategies they can use to develop their ideas. These are sometimes called **rhetorical modes** and include:

- Definition
- Comparison/contrast
- Division/classification
- Examples
- Causal analysis

Depending on the course and instructor you are taking, you might be asked to develop an entire essay using one of these methods. In most academic writing, however, it is more typical for students to use a variety of approaches.

For example, in "Change the Channel," the student has used a variety of these methods, including:

Definition—using the example of the underlying message in beer commercials to explain what is meant by the term "subliminal."
Comparison/contrast—comparing Howard Stern's open handling of sexuality with the more conservative treatment of the subject by more traditional radio personalities.

Division/classification—dividing radio personalities into newscasters, political reporters, smooth talking "stoner dudes" and shock jocks like Howard Stern.

Examples—using specific examples throughout the essay, including the KKK leader and other specific topics discussed on Stern's show.

Causal analysis—making the point that Stern's handling of formerly taboo subjects opened the door for more mainstream media to discuss the same subjects.

Notice, too, that the student incorporated these different rhetorical modes smoothly into an essay whose overall purpose is to explain a concept—in this case, the value of the student's subject.

Chapter Nine: Developing an Essay That Responds to a Text

Aside from essay assignments that ask you to explain an idea or phenomenon, another common type of writing assignment asks you to respond to ideas presented in another work. In some cases, you may be asked to write in response to a novel that has been assigned in your English class; at other times, the book you are reading will be a work of non-fiction that examines interesting ideas and presents the author's views on them. Alternately, you may find your instructor assigns a film and asks you to write about the ideas presented in it. Other examples of texts you may be asked to write about could include advertisements, websites, and even songs. Essentially, anything that is **analyzed** in an essay is being treated as a text, and your instructor could assign almost anything for you to focus on (more on **analysis** later).

Typically, students may also be asked to write about more than one such text, putting the ideas of both together to support a point the student writer is making.

Reading for Ideas

Before you can begin putting together an essay in response to a text, you need to read or view it carefully and look for interesting ideas in it. If you have been assigned a specific topic (like a book's handling of race or gender issues), then make sure you read with a careful eye, paying attention to things that relate to the topic. As you start reading, consider the active reading strategies explained in Chapter One. Previewing a text may be difficult with a novel, but it can still be done, and you should definitely annotate the text you are working with, taking notes on examples and ideas that relate to the themes focused on in your writing assignment. If your copy of the book came from the library or should not be written in for some other reason, a good alternative is to write your annotations on Post-It notes or something similar; stick your notes on the page as you work with the book, and then remove them when you're done with it.

If you have not been assigned a specific topic, but instead have been asked to find your own topic within the text, your task may be a bit more challenging. The best thing to do in this situation is to focus on what interests you the most. Look for themes or related ideas within the text, and think about ways you can relate those ideas to your own experiences or observations. Class discussions of the reading can also be helpful in pointing out themes and key ideas that you may see as worthy subjects to write about. Once you have decided on a theme that appeals to you, keep focused on that idea as you read the text and take good notes to remind you later of parts of the book that struck you as important or interesting as you read.

The same strategies can be applied to a film or other text you may be assigned to write about. Look for patterns and themes that relate to the writing assignment or the topic you have decided on and take notes while watching the film. If possible, watch the film more than once so you can catch important details on a second viewing that you may have missed the first time around.

Writing and Thinking Analytically

Analysis is a process in which we break a text down into its parts and then examine the parts individually, drawing conclusions about their significance to the whole text or the way it makes meaning. If you have previously written an essay explaining a concept (as in Chapter 8), you have already engaged in analysis to some degree. The student who wrote about Howard Stern was analyzing the show by focusing only on some of its parts and making points about their significance.

When working with a text, thinking analytically about it will help you considerably as you begin turning your thoughts into Invention and the beginnings of your essay. Consider the following text, a short version of a children's story familiar to many:

Little Red Riding Hood

Once there was a little girl who wore a red cloak with a hood. She liked it so much that people called her "Little Red Riding Hood." One day, her mother gave her a basket of food and told her to take it to her grandmother's house. The girl's grandmother was ill, and the girl's mother told her it was important to get the food to her. She instructed her daughter to go straight to the grandmother's house, not to leave the path, and not to talk to strangers along the way. But on the way to her grandmother's, Red Riding Hood left the path for a moment and there she saw a wolf, who was very interested in the basket. He asked where she was going, and the girl told him all about her grandmother and what was in the basket. The wolf decided to take a shortcut through the forest and got to the grandmother's house first. He ate the grandmother, put on her clothes and got into her bed. When Red Riding Hood arrived, she was fooled into thinking that the wolf was her grandmother. "What big eyes you have, grandmother," she said. "The better to see you with," said the wolf in disguise. "And what big ears you have," said Red. "The better to hear you with," said the wolf. "And what big teeth you have," said Red. "The better to eat you with!" shouted the wolf as he jumped from the bed and attacked the girl. A passing woodcutter heard Red's screams and entered the house just as the wolf was swallowing the girl. The woodcutter used his axe to cut open the wolf's stomach, freeing Red Riding Hood and her grandmother and killing the wolf.

Analysis of this story might yield several different ideas. By looking at the individual parts of the story, we could come up with several points:

- This is a story that teaches children not to talk to strangers. By failing to listen to her mother's warning, Red Riding Hood put herself and her grandmother in danger.
- This story teaches women and girls that they must do as they are told. Straying from the path is shown to be dangerous, and the women in the story are not strong enough to fight off their attacker.

- This story teaches that men are problem solvers and women are victims. The woodcutter is the only one who is strong enough to kill the wolf.

- This story teaches that violence is an effective way to solve problems. Without the violence of cutting the wolf open, there would be no happy ending.

Notice that these four ideas could be expanded upon and explained in context with other ideas and examples. Also notice that these ideas focus on just two elements of the story: the girl straying from the path and the woodcutter's actions at the end of the story. Other analytical points could likely be drawn from different parts of the story. In writing analytically, the parts of the text that don't fit with the writer's theme don't need to be discussed—unless they clearly contradict what the writer is trying to say.

Your Turn

Consider one of these children's stories and make a short list of details that you remember from it:

- The Three Little Pigs
- Hansel and Gretel
- Snow White and the Seven Dwarves
- Cinderella
- Jack and the Beanstalk

Alternately, if none of these stories strikes you as particularly memorable, list the details from a different story, fairy tale, or children's film.

Once you have come up with a list of details, write an analytical paragraph in which you focus on just one or two meaningful details and write about their significance. Consider the message or lessons these parts of the story may have sent to children—whether intentional or not—and the effects the story may have had on those children.

How to "Read" a Film

When we watch films for entertainment or amusement, we don't often think analytically about what we're seeing. However, when you are assigned a film as part of a writing course and are expected to write about it, you need to approach your viewing of it a bit differently. It is extremely important that you take notes during the film, and if possible you should try to watch it more than once. Just as you would read a novel looking for main ideas, themes, or significant moments that can be related to a bigger idea, you should also look for the same "big ideas" when watching a film. Keep in mind that you will be writing analytically about the film, so you will need to be able to recall specific, detailed examples to draw conclusions about in the same way that you pulled key moments out of a fairy tale in the exercise on the previous page. If your instructor has given you a specific topic, make sure to look for moments in the film that relate to the topic.

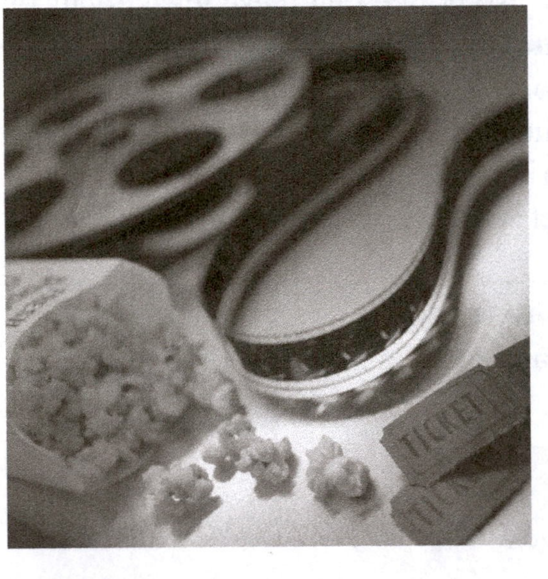

Just like novels, most popular films develop their characters and themes through portraying a series of events. In the first *Star Wars* film, for instance, we first see Luke Skywalker as an excitable farm boy who, through the scenes that follow, develops into a well-trained warrior who takes on a powerful enemy. As you watch a plot unfold, remember that you are looking for specific details that you can write about, so try to resist the temptation to watch the film strictly to be entertained.

It is especially important to note how a film ends and what the outcomes are for the various characters. Ask yourself who prospers and who suffers, which characters succeed and which ones fail, and how you think the filmmakers want viewers to see these characters and their outcomes. For instance, in *Once Were Warriors*, a movie from New Zealand portraying the struggles of a Maori family, the filmmakers depict domestic violence in an extremely graphic way. In one scene, a man viciously attacks a thug in a nightclub, effectively "teaching him a lesson" for being rude to one of the man's friends; viewers may start out cheering the attacker because the thug seems to "deserve" being put in his place. However, when the attack becomes extreme, viewers may start to second-guess their loyalty to the attacker. Later, when the same man's violence is aimed at his wife—whom viewers have already been made to sympathize with—there is no doubt that the attacker is the film's villain. Though viewers may have seen him as something of a hero in the earlier nightclub scene, their loyalty shifts away from him by the film's ending—which makes a statement about violence and the destructiveness that comes from it.

Your Turn

Consider a film you have seen recently. Take some notes on the film's ending and the outcomes of the main characters. Who lives and who dies? Do the lovers end up together? Do characters somehow "pay" for their actions? Which characters are you left to identify with the most? Why? In a paragraph, explain how the characters' outcomes suggest a broader message or lesson that the filmmakers may want viewers to take away. Use specific examples from the film to support your point.

Analyzing Other Images

Just as analytical points can be made about films—which are series of images—so can we write analyses of single images. Again, your task is to look for the ideas or messages being presented by the image, and in writing about advertisements and other images, your job is to explain what you think and why you think it. It is entirely possible for two viewers to find different messages in the same image—just as opinions can differ on the significance of films, fairy tales, novels, or any other text.

Looking at images can be challenging, though, since they are static. That is, there is no movement, no progression from one scene to the next. So instead of looking for movement or character development, you need to look carefully at all the parts of the image. Ask yourself what seems to be the dominant part of the image, the thing your eye is most drawn toward. Using this as a starting point, ask yourself what you think or feel about this dominant element of the image. Now consider what else is happening in the image—other figures, background images, any text that may be part of the image, etc.—and how those other elements of the image correspond to, complement, or contradict the thoughts you had about the dominant part of the image. If the image includes people, look at their eyes. Do they look at the camera or somewhere else?

Studying all these elements of an image can lead you to make interesting analytical points about it. Remember that in doing so, you focus only on specific parts rather than the whole image.

Consider this famous photograph by Dorothea Lange, who captured the image of a migrant mother and her children during the Dust Bowl migration of the 1930s. The woman herself dominates the image, and it is her face more than anything that we focus on, especially her eyes. Notice that she does not look at the camera but rather stares off into the distance, perhaps looking at something specific, or else looking at nothing in particular but just lost in thought. Her brow is wrinkled, and her face could be read as expressing concern, worry, determination, or all three. The dominant part of the image expresses a blend of strength and vulnerability. When we consider the woman's two children and the fact that they look away from the camera, it adds to the

vulnerability portrayed in the image, but we could also "read" the children's posture as revealing more about the mother's strength. They may be frightened of the camera or just trying to hide or rest; in any case, though, they seem to be taking comfort from their mother, which adds to viewers' sense that this woman is strong and capable in the face of her troubles.

These are just some of the ideas that could be worked on in writing analytically about this image—which is not the same as writing a description of it. Remember that in this kind of writing—whether you are focusing on a book, a movie, an image, or some other text, your job is to make and support a point about the meaning or significance of the text, not just to explain what happens in it.

Your Turn

Look through a magazine and find an advertisement that strikes you as interesting. Take some notes on the images in the ad and then write an analytical paragraph in which you use specific examples to explain who seems to be the target audience for the ad and what the advertisers are doing to appeal to that audience. How do they "sell" the product—making it seem attractive, desirable, or necessary? Do the advertisers assume anything about their target audience's views, morals, or values? Be specific in your analysis, and remember that the points you make must be supported by evidence within the image.

Using Quotations

Sometimes, you will find it useful to quote from the text you are writing about, and you may even find that your instructor requires quotations in your essay. Quoting from a text you are analyzing can be extremely useful in showing your reader (who may not be as familiar with the text as you are) exactly what the author wrote and how the author's words correspond to the point you're making. However, you should quote sparingly. If you quote too much, you run the risk of turning your paper into a series of words written by someone else with very little written by you. This does not go over well with most instructors.

When quoting, remember that you should not put a quotation into your paragraph just for the sake of doing it. Even if you are required to quote, you still must not simply place any random quotation from the text into your essay. Instead, **look for a quotation that either directly supports the point you are making or illustrates in a particularly effective way a point being made by the author of the text you are writing about.**

Let's say you have been assigned the book, *John Barleycorn, or Alcoholic Memoirs* by Jack London. You need to write an essay that responds analytically to some aspect of London's book, which is a memoir about his experiences with alcohol (which he refers to as "John Barleycorn") from the age of 5 to adulthood. Toward the end of the book, London writes this paragraph:

> We have with great success made a practice of not leaving arsenic and strychnine, and typhoid and tuberculosis germs lying around for our children to be destroyed by. Treat John Barleycorn the same way. Stop him. Don't let him lie around, licensed and legal, to pounce upon our youth. Not of alcoholics nor for alcoholics do I write, but for our youths, for those who possess no more than the adventure-stings and the genial predispositions, the social man-impulses, which are twisted all awry by our barbarian civilization which feeds them poison on all the corners. It is the healthy, normal boys, now born or being born, for whom I write.

London essentially argues that alcohol should be banned in order to save future generations from the dangers of alcoholism. In writing analytically about this text, let's suppose you choose to focus on just a portion of the above paragraph: "Treat John Barleycorn the same way. Stop him. Don't let him lie around, licensed and legal, to pounce upon our youth." The quotation works well because it is clearly written and forceful; rather than just write "ban alcohol" which would not be all that memorable, London makes alcohol seem like a malevolent force that must be stopped before it destroys more youths.

When quoting, it is extremely important that you do so smoothly, blending your language with that of the person you are quoting. Do this by using an **acknowledging phrase** like "London writes" or "the author argues." Failing to do so will make the paragraph choppy and confusing. Compare the following two paragraphs. Which one uses the quotation more effectively?

Version 1

After describing throughout the book his many years of drinking, London concludes that the way to save young people from the horrors of alcoholism would be to ban liquor altogether. "Treat John Barleycorn the same way. Stop him. Don't let him lie around, licensed and legal, to pounce upon our youth." On its surface, this makes basic sense. If we banned alcohol, it could not harm as many people. However, in his suggestion that alcohol is a predator that waits to "pounce" on its victim, London fails to acknowledge that some people are able to resist alcohol, or at least can resist drinking to excess. Some people may be victims waiting to be pounced on, but others are strong enough to make alcohol a mere amusement. It is unfair that everyone be forbidden from drinking just because some people cannot control themselves.

Version 2

After describing throughout the book his many years of drinking, London concludes that the way to save young people from the horrors of alcoholism would be to ban liquor altogether. Reasoning that outlawing opium has saved many from becoming opium addicts, London writes that society should "Treat John Barleycorn the same way. Stop him. Don't let him lie around, licensed and legal, to pounce upon our youth." On its surface, this makes basic sense. If we banned alcohol, it could not harm as many people. However, in his suggestion that alcohol is a predator that waits to "pounce" on its victim, London fails to acknowledge that some people are able to resist alcohol, or at least can resist drinking to excess. Some people may be victims waiting to be pounced on, but others are strong enough to make alcohol a mere amusement. It is unfair that everyone be forbidden from drinking just because some people cannot control themselves.

You should have noted that the use of the quotation in Version 1 is choppy. Inclusion of the acknowledging phrase "London writes" in Version 2 along with smoothly incorporating the quotation into the student's sentence makes the quotation much more effective. Also note that the writer doesn't simply include the quotation and then move on to other points. Instead, the student analyzes the quotation, showing how London's point relates to the student's own. Remember that if you are required to quote, or simply choose to, you must use the quoted material effectively and as part of your analysis.

Summarizing

When writing analytically about a text—be it a novel, a non-fiction book, a film, or anything else, being able to write effective summaries is key to your success. When you summarize, you give your reader a sense of the **main ideas** in the text without letting yourself get bogged down in the little details. This is important because your summaries will provide your readers with a clear understanding of what you are writing about, especially if those readers are not familiar with the text you have chosen. Even in situations where the whole class writes about the same book or film, or where you know your instructor has read the book you are writing about, you should still assume that your readers don't know the specific parts of the text you're going to focus on as well as you do. Thus, you must provide effective summaries in order for the reader to see your point.

An earlier example in this chapter referenced the first *Star Wars* film. Here is an *ineffective* summary of that movie:

> The film *Star Wars* opens with a small ship being pursued by a much larger one. On board the small ship are a group of rebels, including Princess Leia and two robots—R2D2 and C3PO. On board the larger ship is the film's villain, Darth Vader. Before Vader's troops can capture the princess, she has R2D2 film a holographic image of her in which she sends out a call for help to Obi Wan Kenobi. The two robots escape to the planet Tatooine before Darth Vader can capture them, but he does get the princess. On the planet, the robots are captured by creatures called Jawas, who take them to a farm where Luke Skywalker lives with his aunt and uncle. The Skywalkers buy the robots, and Luke accidentally discovers the

> princess's distress call. When R2D2 escapes, Luke guesses he has gone to find an old man named Ben Kenobi who lives in the desert and who might have something to do with the Obi Wan Kenobi in the holograph. Luke is interested in all of this because he is bored by his life on the farm, and he thinks the princess is beautiful….

This could go on and on. A student writing this sort of thing is giving readers the entire plot of the film rather than summarizing key points. Remember that your goal in writing analytically is to focus on specific parts of a text and make points about them that support an idea of your own. Getting bogged down in all the details of a text turns your writing into a report on the text rather than an analysis in which you have something interesting to say.

Here is a better, more effective summary of the same film.

> This science fiction film is about a group of rebels trying to defeat an evil galactic empire. To defeat the evil forces, the hero, a farm boy named Luke Skywalker, must learn the ways of a nearly extinct group of fighters called Jedi Knights. With the help of an old Jedi, friendly robots, a clever smuggler and his hairy companion, Luke leaves his little planet to go on a quest to rescue a princess and save the galaxy from the Death Star, a huge space ship that can destroy whole planets. By channeling the "force" that he has learned from the old Jedi, Luke succeeds where others have failed, and the rebels are safe from their enemies for the time being.

Of course, there are lots of details left out of this summary, and it does not give readers a clear sense of everything that happens, but it does give us a general sense of what to expect, who the main characters are, and what the film's main themes and ideas are. This would give readers a good understanding of the film and enable them to see the point that the student writer is making about it without having to know about everything that happens.

Your Turn

The short summary of *Star Wars* above is 122 words long. Choose a film you have seen recently and write a summary of it that is no more than 125 words. Remember to focus just on the main events and key ideas in the film to help a reader who has not seen it get a clear understanding of what happens in it.

Using Summary and Analysis Together

Typically, you will not need to summarize a whole film or a whole book when writing an analytical essay in response to a text. Instead, you will usually need to summarize parts of the text to use as examples supporting the point you make in your analysis.

Let's take another film as an example. Imagine that a student has been asked to identify and explain one of the messages in Spike Jonze's film adaptation of the children's book, *Where the Wild Things Are*. The student has come up with this thesis: In *Where the Wild Things Are*, the filmmakers send a message that adults often fail to see the devastating effects their words and actions can have on children; the film suggests that when children act out, adults should try to understand them rather than punish them.

In putting together a body paragraph in support of this thesis, the student would need specific examples from the film and analysis of those examples to show how they support his or her point. Here is what one body paragraph might look like:

Topic sentence and transition into the main example.

Summary of the scene in the classroom.

Before Max goes off to join the wild things, we see several short scenes portraying the sources of his frustration. One that goes on a bit longer than the others shows Max's teacher explaining to a room of children that the sun will eventually burn out. He describes this in detail, apparently unaware that this may be frightening the children. In a poor attempt at softening the harsh reality, he also explains that humans will likely die out before the sun does, wiped out by global catastrophe, disease, etc. Along with portrayals of Max's broken family, his mother's flirtations with her new boyfriend, and his sister's rejection of him, this scene in the classroom shows us another aspect of the instability in Max's life—it seems as though the whole universe is against him and that he can't count on anything, not even the sun. The scene is later echoed when Carol, Max's best friend among the wild things on the island, expresses fear that the sun has burned out. Like Max, Carol also just wants his "family" to all get along and to stay together, and his expressions of rage over the instability of his world are frightening and understandable. The two scenes complement each other and show viewers that Max's outbursts should be just as fully sympathized with as Carol's; they may not be excusable or appropriate, but simple understanding of the boy's difficulties could make his situation a bit easier.

Analysis of the classroom scene.

Summary of another scene on the island.

Analysis of how the scenes work together to illustrate the writer's point.

When writing an entire essay in response to one or two texts, you need to select effective examples and be able to write about them in enough detail to make the essay interesting and believable. You also need to balance your use of summary and analysis, being careful not to go overboard with the summary and start describing everything that happens in a book or movie.

The following is a student-written essay in response to two texts. The student was assigned a novel, *Bread Givers* by Anzia Yezierska, a book from 1925 that portrays the life of an immigrant Jewish girl struggling to survive in New York City and get an education in spite of the barriers put up by her culture and her domineering father. Along with this book, the student also watched a film, *Real Women Have Curves*, which is about a young Latina trying to break free from familial and cultural restrictions to find her own way in more modern Los Angeles. Notice how the student blends summary of key moments in the book and movie with analysis of those examples to show how they support the points she is making.

Overcoming Obstacles

From applications to exams, college can be a complete nightmare to most students and one of the most challenging experiences someone can go through.

However, the struggles of most students are nothing compared to what a first-generation college student would go through. Wanting to go to college is one thing, but understanding the process is another. Many students who are the first ones from their family attending college often approach many difficulties, such as not receiving support from their families and not being able to afford college. Reading the novel, *Bread Givers*, and watching the film, *Real Women Have Curves*, gives people the opportunity to fully understand how hard it is to be a first-generation college student through the lives of two young women named Ana and Sara.

One of the main reasons why it is more difficult for a first-generation college student opposed to a student who has had family members attend college, would be the support. In most cases, first-generation college students don't receive as much support from their families as they should, or even none at all. Ana, from *Real Women Have Curves*, comes from a lower-class Hispanic family who views college as a waste of time. Her mother believes she can teach Ana everything she needs to know. Cooking, cleaning, and taking care of her future family are what Ana's mother views as the most important things her daughter can learn in order to succeed in life. Not only does Ana not get support from her family, but they also use guilt against her, holding her responsible for helping in her sister's sweatshop or accusing her of wanting to leave her grandfather all alone by going off to college. All of this discourages Ana, and throughout most of the film it seems that she will give in to their desire to see her stay home and not pursue her education. Eventually, though, she ignores her mother's wishes and decides to go with her dream of going to college after being encouraged by one of her high school teachers, Mr. Guzman. His character shows viewers that first generation students often need to look for support and encouragement from outside their families.

When it comes to family support, Sara's life isn't much different at all. Sara comes from a lower-class Jewish family living on Hester Street in New York in the early 1900s. Sara's father, who is an Orthodox Jew, believes women will go to Heaven, "…if they cooked for the men, and washed for the men, and didn't hag or curse the men out of their homes; only if they let the men study the Torah in peace, then, maybe, they would push themselves into Heaven with the men, to wait on them there." This quotation shows that Sara's father is sexist and sees women as only meant to serve men, which means going to college would be out of the question. After arguing with her father for several years, Sara decides to run away and survive by herself while going to college. During her years of attending college, Sara has many visits from her family. First, her mother argues with Sara about never visiting her while she's going to school and says, "Is college more important than to see your old mother?" Just like Ana, Sara is guilt tripped by her mother, but ends up ignoring it. Fania and Bessie, Sara's sisters, visit her as well and are shocked at what Sara is doing with her life; they want her to marry and start a family. According to them, she's an old maid. With all of this on Sara's mind, it only gets worse. Her next visitor is her father, who ends up disowning her. All of this discourages Sara, making it more difficult for her to focus on her education. However, she is strong-willed and still manages to stay on track, going to college in spite of her family's opposition.

Another reason why it is much harder for a first-generation college student would be how most of these students come from lower-class families who can not afford college tuition. Ana's family all work jobs that don't pay very well. Her family not only sees college as a waste of time, but also a waste of money. Since college is not one of their top priorities, they don't want to pay for it. Because of this, Ana does not even imagine an academic future for herself. Without help and encouragement from Mr. Guzman, she would never have succeeded. Because of him, though, she earns a full scholarship to Columbia, resulting in her family not having to pay for her tuition. Ana's journey to college would have been much easier if she had come from a family like those of her high school classmates, all of whom seemed able to help their children get into college. As a first generation student, Ana had to work much harder to even get out the door and into college. The film ends by showing her strength; she leaves for college independently and knowing what she wants in life.

Sara's family is even worse off than Ana's, with barely enough money to put dinner on the table. None of the girls receives a proper education, and when Sara makes the decision to become a teacher, she must first go to night school to get caught up before she can go to college. Throughout her entire education, she has to work in sweatshops and laundries to pay her expenses and tuition. This makes her struggle much worse than what other students in the book must face. Her fellow students, all coming from families that support their educational goals, do not have to work and have time to study and socialize. Sara must labor every night before going home to do her schoolwork and never has time for nice clothes or socializing with her peers. Not only is she exhausted, but lonely and frustrated, and her situation as a first generation student often makes her want to quit. Like Ana, though, she does not give up. Struggling to support herself, Sara ends up graduating and becomes a teacher without the help or support from her family.

From all the struggles first-generation students face going into college, they still can have the same outcome as any other student who has had family members attend college. They just encounter a lot more obstacles that they must overcome to succeed. These obstacles make them much stronger in life. From watching and reading the lives of Ana and Sara, people can see how they came from families who people would think would never make it; instead they make their dream of going to college happen, and can inspire readers and viewers to make their own academic dreams come true.

Notice that in writing about these two texts, the student had to organize her ideas in what is commonly called a **comparison/contrast** essay. When writing this sort of essay, in which you make points about the similarities and differences between two subjects, you need to make certain that you have a strong thesis that **clearly has something to say about the similarities and differences** rather than just identifying what those similarities and differences are. In other words, it would not be as strong an essay if the thesis simply stated that these two characters' struggles are largely the same. This would probably get a huge "So What?" from most readers. Instead, the writer has made a point about what these students' struggles can tell us about the challenges that first generation college students often face.

How you **organize** your essay is another thing to consider when writing about two subjects like this. Notice that the student focused on specific points—lack of family support and lack of financial support—and that she wrote about both subjects in the same order: starting with *Real Women Have Curves* and then *Bread Givers* in both sections of the essay. Sticking to a pattern is useful since it helps the reader follow the essay's logic more easily. The student could also have organized her essay around each text rather than the different subjects. In this case, she would have written about the film, using all her examples of family and financial support before going on to discuss the novel and the examples from it in the same order. In either case, the essay would work well and be easily followed. How you organize your essay is up to you; the most important thing is that you do have a plan for organizing it and that you stick to it.

Chapter Ten: Developing an Essay That Argues

In some ways, we could consider everything we write for an academic audience to be some sort of an argument. In writing a remembered event essay, a student needs to persuade readers that the events really happened and that they had a particular meaning for the writer. In an expository essay, a student needs to persuade readers of the validity of his or her interpretation or understanding of the subject or its significance. In both cases, this can be achieved through the use of specific, detailed examples and thorough, logical analysis of them.

However, when asked specifically to write an essay that argues, you need to change your focus a bit. When writing an essay that argues or persuades, it is even more important that you keep your audience in mind. If you **focus on the idea that your reader disagrees with you** or, at the very least, is skeptical of the ideas you are presenting, it will help you write a stronger, more persuasive essay. You should assume that your audience is composed of reasonable people who may be familiar with your subject, but who do not see it the same way that you do. While you may not be able to persuade such an audience to change its mind and come over to your way of thinking, you can at least show that your ideas are valid and reasonable.

More than in any other writing situation, it is crucial that your thesis present a clear, opinionated point of view, that it is lively and interesting, and that it is based on sound thinking that you have done in preparation for writing. Arriving at such a thesis and writing a solid essay that supports it requires you to put considerable thought into your subject before you begin writing.

Structuring Your Argument

When putting together an argument, it may be helpful for you to think of your thesis as the essay's **claim**. In other words, you will be claiming in the essay that something is good or bad, right or wrong, helpful or harmful, should or should not be done, etc. Whatever claim you arrive at, assume your readers hold a contrary claim. Once you have decided on a claim, you will need to think about how best to **support** it. This is crucial in an argument. If everyone agreed with your claim, you wouldn't need support for it, but since your audience disagrees, you must provide something to back the claim.

Support generally takes two forms in persuasive essays:

- Evidence
- Appeals

Oftentimes, there will not be a clear line dividing these types of support, and you may find that you use evidence as part of an appeal or that the language used to describe your evidence causes it to function as an appeal as well.

Evidence. In the Declaration of Independence, Thomas Jefferson made a claim that the American colonies had the right to declare their independence from Great Britain because the British government had abused the colonists' rights in a variety of ways. Jefferson then went on to list those abuses in very specific language. This was the evidence he used to support his claim. In writing a persuasive essay, you will need to include various types of evidence to support your claim. These can take several forms:

- Examples, personal or otherwise.
- Facts
- Statistics
- Expert testimony

Try to include a variety of evidence. Writers of strongly persuasive essays rely on more than just personal examples or just straight facts and statistics since they realize there is considerable variety among their audience members. Try to cast a wide net, using as many types of evidence as is practical in order to persuade the greatest number of readers.

You should also make certain that the evidence you include is **relevant**. That is, if you're writing about childhood obesity and have statistics from 1978 as part of your support, that material will likely weaken your essay since it is probably no longer accurate.

As you work on your essay, you may find that you need to include material from outside sources in order for your evidence to move beyond the purely personal. In some classes, your instructor may supply you with readings to draw from, but there will likely be times when you will need to do some research. There will be more on this in the next chapter.

Appeals. Imagine a family conversation in which teenage girl is trying to convince her parents that she should be allowed to borrow the family car on Saturday night. When she brings up the point that her parents allowed another child in the family to borrow the car the week before, she is appealing to her parents' sense of fairness. That is, everything else being equal, she expects her parents to treat each child in the family the same, and not to practice favoritism. When you write a persuasive essay, you will also appeal to your readers' sense of what is right and wrong, good and bad. You may make emotional appeals as long as they are not overly manipulative (imagine the same teenager trying to use tears to get the car), and you may also appeal to your readers' notion of what makes good sense.

Again, in the Declaration of Independence, Thomas Jefferson lists the many wrongs committed by the British government. These facts serve as evidence, but they also function as an appeal. By explaining that injustices have occurred and that groups of people deserve to be treated justly, Jefferson appeals to his audience's sense of fairness and common ideas of the conditions that need to be met in order for societies to exist and prosper. If his audience had disagreed with him, perhaps feeling that the rights of kings are absolute and not to be questioned, his appeal would not have been as effective.

When writing the first draft of your persuasive essay, take some time to list the evidence and appeals you are using to support your claim. If you find you are using one type of evidence over and over, or that the argument depends more on evidence than appeals, try to add material to make the essay more balanced, and thus more persuasive.

Thinking Critically

The ability to think critically is extremely important to argumentative writing and to academic success in general. Often, students have a negative reaction to the word *critical*, assuming that being criticized is the same as being attacked or put down. When asked to read critically, they think they are being asked to read negatively, to look for weaknesses or flaws in a text. This is not necessarily the case, however. Remember that film critics don't always give bad reviews; rather, a good critic will focus on the parts of a film—characters, plot, dialogue, direction, etc.—and explain how those parts add up to a film we should see or avoid.

In the same way, in your academic work it may be more helpful to view critical thinking as **careful, deliberate thinking** that helps you not only to understand the ideas and opinions you encounter, but also to understand why you agree or disagree with those ideas and what the strengths or weaknesses of someone else's argument may be. Thus, it is important that you begin your work on an argumentative essay by giving yourself the opportunity to think critically about your subject. Rather than accept an idea simply because of how you feel about it, thinking critically about the issue will enable you to explain and defend your position. Sometimes, thinking critically causes us to re-examine our opinions and possibly even change them. As with any kind of writing, this can't happen if you rush the process. Waiting until the night before a draft is due to start coming up with an argument is a sure way to make it weak.

Writing assignments for argument essays usually take one of these forms:

- Take a position on a controversial subject and support your position with specific examples and analysis.
- Explain an argument made by another writer and whether you agree with that author's position. Use specific examples and analysis to show why you agree or disagree.

In some cases, you will be given specific issues or arguments to write about; at other times, instructors give their students more choice to come up with controversial subjects or other writers' opinions on their own. In either case, you need to decide where you stand on the issue before you can put together your own argument on the subject. Engaging in critical thinking can help you develop your ideas.

Here are a few things to consider:

Don't Let Emotions or Biases Cloud Your Judgment. We are all biased in favor of some things and against others, and it is impossible to write an argument without some level of bias in it. Let's say you've been asked to write about same-sex marriage. By saying that you think it should be legal, you are expressing bias toward that view. If you express this bias in a reasonable manner, bringing up examples about equal rights and comparing the issue to other civil rights causes, your argument would likely sound logical and not slanted by your bias. However, if you have arrived at your position simply because the current law makes you angry or sad, and if you present the argument strictly in emotional terms, your views will seem slanted and unreasonably biased. This is not to say that you shouldn't write about things you feel strongly about. Rather, make sure your strong feelings don't take over the essay.

Look at the Assumptions Underlying Your Argument. When developing your thesis, keep in mind the **assumptions** you base your ideas on. These are the sometimes unstated beliefs and opinions that help form your position. If your argument is set up in such a way that it suggests your readers share the same assumptions, then the essay may be severely weakened. For example, a student writing about banning smoking on campus might write a sentence like this: "Smoking is a disgusting, dirty habit, and banning it will only make this campus more beautiful and dignified." When used this way, the words *disgusting, dirty, beautiful* and *dignified* are examples of **loaded language** that attempt to make your argument without offering any support. The writer assumes his or her audience feels the same way about smoking, taking it as given. This is called "begging the question," and there will be more on this later. If the student's reader is a smoker, is good friends with a smoker, is perhaps a former smoker, or simply has no opinion on the issue, then loaded language will likely cause such a reader to react badly to the argument. Now, consider this revision of the sentence above:

> "Because so many smokers toss their cigarette butts on the ground, they cause the campus to look *dirty*, and if one thinks about the germs on those cigarette butts, it is truly *disgusting*. Banning smoking would end such unsanitary littering, making the campus more *dignified* and allowing its *beauty* to be untarnished."

The student has still managed to use the same words but does so now with a more **reasonable** tone, offering support for the judgmental language.

Students who smoke might still disagree with the ideas in the essay, but they would be much less likely to feel personally attacked by the writer. For student writers, a more important fact may be that their instructors watch for this kind of thing. It's not likely that your instructor expects you to write an argument that pleases everyone and alienates no one; rather, your instructor is probably looking to see if you are paying attention to your audience's needs and are constructing an essay that is free of biased assumptions.

Develop Your Essay Around Opinions Rather Than Beliefs. When putting your ideas together, make sure that you build your essay on a sound **opinion** rather than a **belief**. An opinion may be described as a sort of belief, but it is one based on information and facts while pure belief is more often a question of faith or instinct. A student who believes in the existence of extraterrestrial life may argue that the government should spend more money attempting to make contact with such beings. However, an argument based on this belief—without any kind of proof that such life exists—would not be strong. Effective essays develop from informed opinions—that is, opinions based on accurate facts and information. Similarly, you don't want to base your argument on individual **taste**. That is, arguing that vanilla is better than chocolate won't get you very far since your audience may feel that chocolate is better than vanilla. The positions on both sides were not arrived at scientifically or through other careful study but rather are just reflections of taste or personal preference. No matter how skilled the arguer, it is not likely that an essay built on this sort of idea will be persuasive.

Use Sound Logic. This may be a bit tricky, since most people think they're being logical even in cases where they're not. Developing a strong sense of logic requires careful, deliberate thinking. We can divide logic into two basic types: **inductive** and **deductive**. An inductive argument moves from specific pieces of evidence, or data, and toward a general conclusion. For example, if you looked at the study habits of most of your peers in this class, you would be able to make an

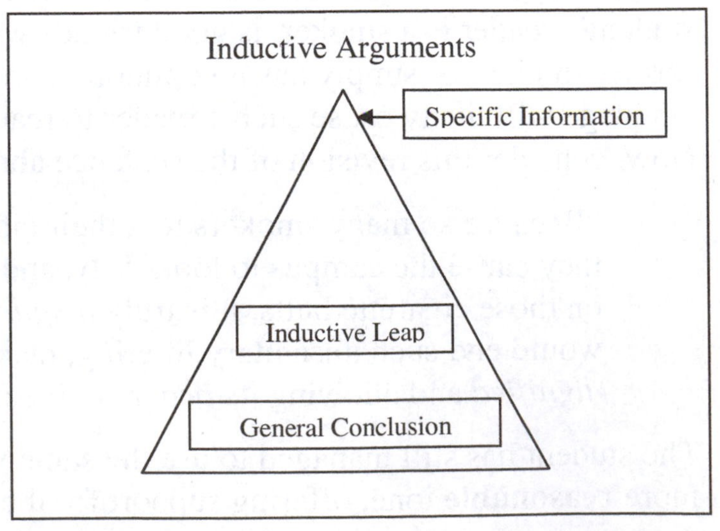

inductive argument about the class's preferences and behaviors. Looking at 20 students and basing a conclusion about the whole class on that data would likely produce a sound argument. But trying to use those same 20 students to make an argument about the whole college or about college students in general would result in an argument with too small a sampling. It would thus have faulty induction. The same problem occurs when a writer relies entirely on personal experience. For example: "Everyone should quit eating chocolate; I quit, and it was good for me, so everyone else would benefit the same way." This, again, is too small a sampling. Just because one person benefited from a particular behavior does not mean that the other 6 billion of us would benefit similarly.

On the other hand, a deductive argument moves from general to specific, using a truth about a large class of things as the basis of an argument, connecting that to a more narrow truth, and then combining the ideas to arrive at a single, specific claim.

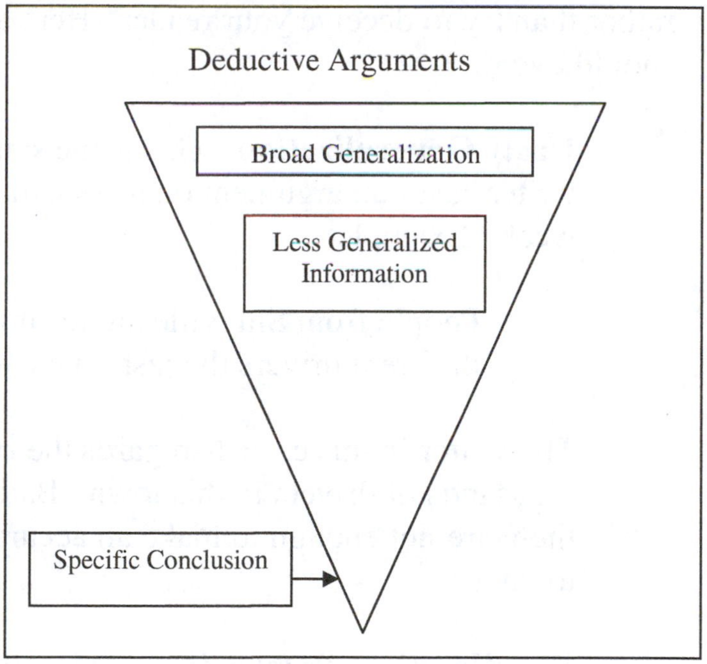

For example:

- Smokers have a high risk for certain diseases.
- Joe is a smoker.
- Therefore, Joe has a high risk for certain diseases.

The problem with this kind of logic occurs when one of the "truths" is actually not true.

For example:

- People who cannot read are ignorant.
- Joe cannot read.
- Therefore, Joe is ignorant.

Looked at uncritically, this argument may make sense. But when we carefully consider the first part of it—People who cannot read are ignorant—we should begin to see some problems. While there *may* be a connection between literacy and intelligence in *some* people, there can be reasons for illiteracy that have nothing to do with intelligence. For example, Joe may not be able to read because he cannot see and has never learned Braille; or perhaps he cannot read because he has never been taught. One would hardly call Joe ignorant because of his reading ability if he was only 2 years old.

Avoid Logical Fallacies. A **fallacy** is a way of thinking that is simply not logical. Some writers fall into the trap of fallacies accidentally because they have not thought through their arguments fully enough or are letting emotion or personal preferences control their writing. Other writers may use fallacies intentionally to confuse, distract, or mislead their readers into thinking a certain way because the actual argument being made is weak and would not stand up to good critical scrutiny. This is not recommended, especially in your academic writing. If your argument doesn't work, fix the argument rather than try to deceive your reader. Here are some common fallacies you should avoid:

Hasty Generalization. This is the same as weak induction. If a writer bases an argument on too small a sampling, the conclusion is weak. Example:

> People from Slugville are terrible drivers. I got cut off by three different drivers the last time I was there.

The writer in this case disregards the fact that there are likely thousands of drivers in this town. Bad experiences with only three of them are not enough to make an accurate judgment about the whole town.

***Post Hoc Ergo Propter Hoc*.** This is Latin for "Before this, therefore because of this." It is basically a faulty cause and effect argument, suggesting that just because one event came before another, the first event caused the second. A lot of superstitious thinking is based on this fallacy. Example:

> Don't let a black cat cross your path. One day, a black cat crossed my path, and a few minutes later I tripped and broke my ankle.

This writer blames the cat for the broken ankle rather than looking at a more likely cause—the writer's own clumsiness.

Begging the Question. This fallacy was discussed earlier with the example about smokers. A writer who begs the question is putting forth an idea as though it were true and without question, essentially begging the reader to accept it unconditionally. If the assumptions behind the fact are shaky, then the fact itself becomes questionable. Example:

> Vote for Measure X and save the children.

Regardless of what Measure X is, the writer here takes it as given that the children need saving and that the audience agrees with this.

False Dilemma. In presenting this sort of argument, the writer suggests that there are only two choices in a given situation; furthermore, one choice is always made to look far worse than the other, supporting the idea that failing to support the writer's ideas will lead to problems. Example:

> The district's extra 20 million dollars must go to teachers' salaries. We can either pay them more to teach, or find that we are losing our best teachers to other districts.

Here, the writer suggests that there is no other choice. Without better pay, teachers will not stay in the district. The problem is that there may be other options, such as using the 20 million dollars to improve facilities, upgrade technology, improve benefits, etc., all of which could make staying in the district an attractive option for teachers.

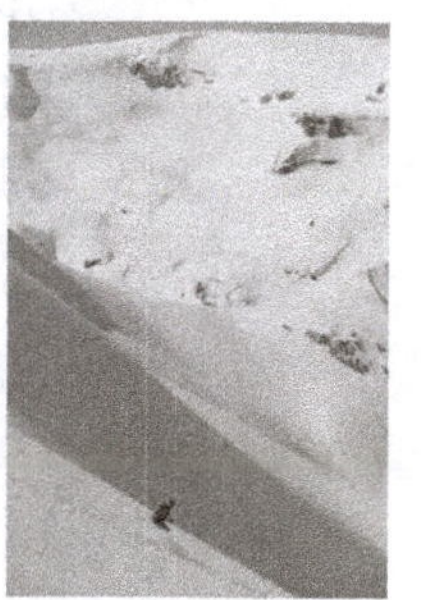

Slippery Slope. Here, the writer suggests that if one thing happens, a series of unpleasant things will follow, leading to disaster. Imagine someone standing on the edge of an ice-covered hill. One step in the wrong direction sends the person to the bottom of the slippery slope with no hope for recovery. Example:

> We must not restrict the content of the Internet. If we censor Internet content, we will soon find ourselves in a repressive, fascist state similar to Nazi Germany.

This is faulty logic. The writer assumes that regulating one area of society will lead to a complete change without taking into consideration all of the factors that led to repression in Nazi Germany or the ways that controlling the Internet would lead to increased censorship in other parts of society.

Ad Hominem. This is Latin for "against the man" and describes an argument that takes the form of a personal attack against the opposition rather than focusing on the issues or the weaknesses in the opposition's argument. Example:

> Dalton Trumbo's anti-war message in *Johnny Got His Gun* should not be listened to since the author was a communist.

Here, a writer's political ideology is being attacked rather than the substance of his argument.

Ad Populum. This is Latin for "appeal to the people" and asserts that something must be true or good because the majority of the population feels this way. This overlooks the fact that many people do things even though they're wrong, or that the preferences of the masses may be based on inaccurate information, purely emotional responses, or other things that may not provide sound logical bases for an argument. Example:

> There is nothing wrong with downloading songs or movies without paying for them. Hundreds of thousands of people do it without ever getting punished.

Even though many people engage in an illegal activity, this does not make it morally or ethically acceptable.

Appeal to Tradition. Like the *ad populum* argument, an argument that uses an appeal to tradition tries to argue that if others feel something is right, then it must be right. In this case, those who agree with a claim are people from the past. Example:

> The trend of moving toward hybrid vehicles is ridiculous. Generations of drivers have relied on standard gasoline engines in their cars, and there is no reason to think that what worked in the past can no longer work today.

Someone making this argument fails to see that changes in technology or society or the environment could make the old way of doing things obsolete or impractical.

Appeal to Emotion. There may be times when using emotionally loaded language can be useful and effective in an argument. However, when an argument uses emotional language for purposes of being manipulative, it is no longer logical. Example:

> Raising college tuition will only place a greater burden on honest, hardworking students who want nothing more than a chance to succeed in the harsh, cruel environment of modern society.

While the students may be honest and hardworking, and while society may be harsh and cruel, the argument over tuition likely has more to do with budgets and the costs of operating a college, factors that are overlooked when the language becomes too emotional.

Straw Man. This refers to the practice of setting up an opposing view and then pointing out its weaknesses. If done well, this can actually be an effective strategy in an argument (more on this later). However, when the opposing view is distorted by the arguer, it only *looks* like an opposing view and thus is part of a fallacious argument. Imagine how much easier it would be to knock over a straw man instead of a real one. Example:

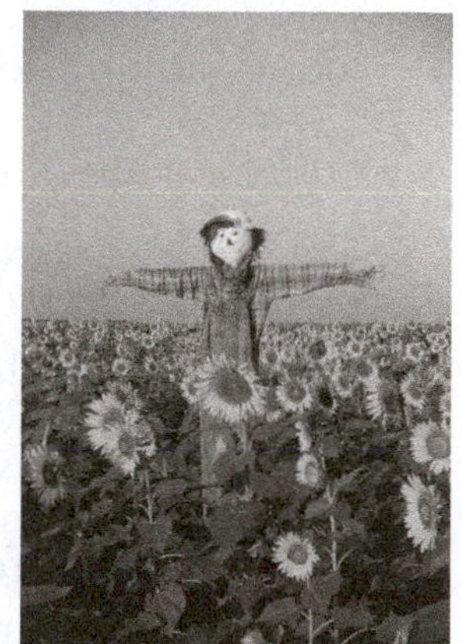

> Those in favor of bilingual education are trying to undermine the English language and all of the traditions that come from it. We should not support bilingual education in any circumstances.

This writer disregards the fact that many proponents of bilingual education seek to improve the skills of non-Native speakers by including education in their native languages. Misrepresenting the opposition is not a logical way of supporting one's own position.

Red Herring. Imagine a criminal who has escaped from prison; the guards pursue the prisoner with dogs. To throw the dogs off the scent, the escapee drags a fish across the trail to distract the dogs. This is basically the same thing that happens with the "red herring" in an argument. The arguer will add an element to the argument that only seems relevant but which is really designed to distract readers and get them to think about an unrelated issue. Example:

> Traditional grading systems should be abolished. Low grades hurt students' self-esteem, which makes them perform more poorly overall. So getting rid of the grading system would improve self-esteem and overall academic performance.

By connecting grades to self-esteem, the arguer tries to divert readers from the broader argument of the value of grades, or their lack of value.

Your Turn

Explain the faulty logic in each of these statements:

1. Mom, if you loved me, you'd let me borrow your car this weekend.
2. The senator's proposal should be defeated. After all, he has admitted to being an adulterer, and we would not want a man with such loose morals to guide and shape our society.
3. Of course I'm voting for the Republican this election. My parents and grandparents have always voted Republican.
4. She must be a witch. I saw her talking to a black cat on Friday the 13th.
5. My opponent feels that all cats and dogs should be spayed and neutered. This clearly infringes on the freedom of choice of many pet owners, and I would encourage you not to vote for someone who values freedom so little.

6. We must defeat the bill to increase the speed limit to 70 miles per hour on our freeways. If we pass this increase, more will follow, and soon there will be no speed limit at all.
7. We can either move toward tougher penalties on music piracy, or we will see the end of recorded music as we know it.
8. Once you've seen one slasher film, you've seen them all.
9. The writer is a woman and thus a feminist. We should consider her opinions carefully.

Critically Evaluating Another Argument

In some situations, you may be asked to write an argumentative essay on a topic of your choice based solely on your opinions and experiences. Quite often, though, argumentative writing will be based on your response to a **text**—an article, an essay, a book, a speech, or possibly some other sort of non-written text like an advertisement, a film, a work of art, etc. Critically approaching a text can also give a reader insight into the writer's approach, his or her biases, the reasons the text was produced, etc.

Thinking critically involves getting past your own biases and emotional responses to a text or idea. Rather than looking for what you agree or disagree with in a text, look for the things an author does to make you agree or disagree, and be open to the idea that you may disagree with the main idea in an essay while still giving its author credit for having constructed a sound argument.

When you think critically about a text, you need to engage in the following processes:

- Consider the conditions under which the text was written
- Examine the author's relationship with his/her audience
- Carefully analyze the structure of the text
- Question how effectively the author presents his/her material

Finally, you will need to arrive at an **evaluation** of the text in which you put your observations together.

Consider the conditions under which the text was written. Before reading, get as much information as you can about the text and its author. If you are reading an essay in an anthology, carefully read any introductory material and check the Acknowledgements page to see when the essay was written and where it was originally published. This can give you some sense of what the author's original intention was as well as his or her original audience. An essay on drugs that originally appeared in a magazine like *High Times* would likely have a different audience and purpose than an essay published in *Time* or *Newsweek.* Understanding this could give you a clearer sense of what the author is trying to achieve as well as the strengths and weaknesses of the essay.

Examine the author's relationship with his/her audience. This requires you to get a sense of the author's tone of voice. Does the author come across as friendly or threatened, as an authority or as someone exploring ideas, as a serious scholar or an amused observer? Some writers assume a hostile perspective; others assume they are writing for people who already agree with them. Understanding a writer's relationship with his or her audience can help students see what the writer assumes of that audience. If an author makes a general statement without offering support, this may indicate that the author assumes readers will agree, but this may not be true, and it may suggest a problem in the essay's logic. For instance, if an author writes, "Everyone understands the importance of family," the "everyone" to whom the author refers may actually be people in the essay's original intended audience. When the same essay is reproduced in an anthology to be used in a college classroom, the audience is not the same, and it is possible for readers to imagine audience members who may not have the same view of "family" as the author assumed. This could then be looked at critically and seen as a potential weakness in the essay.

Carefully analyze the structure of the text. Just as you do with your own writing and that of your peers, you should carefully consider the way an author has put a text together. Look for the text's thesis or main idea and ask yourself how it is supported and developed. If the examples are specific and believable, you may take that as a positive sign of the text's success. If the examples are general or hard to imagine, you may see that as a weakness in the text. Does the essay seem fair in its selection and analysis of examples, or is the author slanting the material in his or her favor unfairly?

Question how effectively the author presents his/her material. Ask yourself how the author is using examples, evidence, facts and statistics in a text. Is the material effectively analyzed? Does an essay rely on humor, sarcasm, or emotionally loaded words and images to get its point across? Ask yourself if these elements of the essay make it effective or not. Did you find yourself moved, challenged, angered, amused, or bored? Do you think your response was what the author intended? You should also take note of the author's logic. Do the conclusions seem sound? Has the author presented him or herself as reasonable? Has the author included any opposing views and explained their weaknesses or their relation to the position being taken? If a text does not strike you as logical, there may be serious weaknesses with it.

Evaluating the Evidence

Once you have spent some time thinking critically about a text, you are ready to evaluate it. In doing so, you are making a claim about its success or failure. You should base such an evaluation on the clarity, structure, logic and tone of the text, taking into consideration the author's intended audience and how the text may be read by a more general audience.

Remember that a critical evaluation should not be based on whether you agree or disagree with the text or with an author's overall message. Imagine that you feel strongly about eliminating junk food in elementary school vending machines. If you read a text that presents this very argument but does so in a weak way, relying on generalizations or overly emotional language that attempts to gain pity for overweight children, you would likely arrive at a negative evaluation, **criticizing the essay for its weaknesses even though you agree with the idea behind it.** Similarly, you could positively evaluate a text that you disagree with on a personal level but which you feel has been written effectively and logically.

Depending on the requirements of your writing assignment, you may have to evaluate one or more texts and base your own view on them, explaining whether you agree or disagree, what the strengths and weaknesses of the text or texts are, and so on.

Opposing Ideas

When developing your argumentative essay, it is extremely important that you take some time to think about **opposing ideas**—points that might be brought up by someone who disagrees with your main idea. You may encounter such ideas in the reading you do in preparation for writing an argumentative essay. It might even be a good idea to write a list of pros and cons related to your subject as part of your invention strategies for such a paper. Not only will this help give you a sense of whom you are trying to convince in your essay, but it will also help you develop your ideas against these opposing points.

Furthermore, strong argumentative essays incorporate opposing ideas and **refute** them, thus poking holes in the other side's arguments.

For example, let's say you're arguing that your college campus should be smoke-free. After giving some thought to possible opposing points of view, you choose one that you think might be commonly held. In a paragraph, briefly explain that position and then explain what is wrong with it, perhaps based on the logic of the opposing view, things that the other side is not taking into consideration when taking this position, etc. Here is what such a paragraph might look like:

Opposing view stated and briefly explained.

Transition from opposing view to the writer's refutation.

Specific examples showing the problems inherent in the opposing view stated earlier.

One group opposed to a smoke-free campus would be students who smoke and who feel that they have the same rights as any other student to engage in legal activities on campus. They have paid their tuition and fees and may even agree to smoke away from buildings and doorways. However, these smokers have not taken into consideration the fact that not all smokers are courteous. Their fellow smokers light up on benches in the quad right outside of classrooms, some of which have their windows open. Other smokers stand right outside of buildings, smoking on their breaks between classes, and the smoke and the smell follow them into the buildings when they go to class. While all students may have the same rights to the space around them, the non-smoker generally does not do anything to invade the space of the smoker, but the smoker, on the other hand, frequently invades the space of others, effectively infringing on the rights of everyone who does not smoke and does not want the smell or the health risks to follow the smoker into a place of higher learning.

When bringing up opposing points of view, make sure you state them briefly. Otherwise, you may be giving the opposing side too much space, effectively weakening your own argument. Instead, give the other side a few sentences, letting the reader know who might hold such an opinion, and follow it with a clear transition that shows you are about to poke holes in the argument you just explained.

Presenting and refuting opposing views accomplishes several things:

- It shows that you are reasonable and rational, having looked at both sides of the issue and come to your position logically.
- It also serves as the writer's acknowledgement that there *is* another side to the argument, thus showing again that you are rational and reasonable.
- Perhaps most importantly, by giving voice to at least some views opposed to the writer's position, he or she shows an awareness that the audience may disagree with the essay's main claim. If a writer fails to bring up any of the audience's positions on the subject, it will likely lead that audience to continue holding those opposing views. But if some of those ideas are brought up and then revealed to be weak in comparison to the author's position, the essay now has a chance at persuading a hostile audience of the validity of the essay's thesis.

There are several ways to **organize** a persuasive essay. One way would be to start with the writer's position, explaining it thoroughly with specific examples and ending with an opposing view and refutation of it. Another method would be to start with an opposing view and let the refutation of it lead into the rest of the author's argument. Still another way of organizing the essay would be to include several opposing views, using them and the author's refutation of them as the means to develop the author's position with each part of it directly related to and in opposition to some other idea. None of these methods are necessarily better than the others. The choice is yours, and the best method for one topic may not be the best for another. Experiment with different organizational strategies to see what will work best for your paper.

The following is a student-written essay in which the author was required to respond to and evaluate an argument by another writer—Gore Vidal's

"Drugs—in which the author advocates the legalization of all drugs. Notice that the student brings up several points from Vidal's essay, even acknowledging that several of them are strong; however, the student writer then points out the flaws in Vidal's argument.

Why Drugs?

In the essay "Drugs," Gore Vidal argues that all drugs should be legalized. He believes that drugs should be made available and sold at cost, and that each drug should be labeled with a description of its effects. Although Vidal brings up some good points, his argument is flawed. Legalizing drugs may produce some positive outcomes at first, but it can potentially have disastrous outcomes in the long run. Many of these drugs can cause physical and psychological damage. Apart from damaging the drug user, drugs can also destroy friendships, families, cities, and even countries.

Vidal begins his essay by stating that there is an easy way to end drug addiction. He writes, "It is possible to stop most drug addiction in the United States within a very short time. Simply make all drugs available and sell them at cost. Label each drug with a precise description of what effect—good and bad—the drug will have on whoever takes it" (196). Vidal brings up a good point. However, taking the easy way out in the present can backfire in the future.

Legalizing drugs and adding a simple description of the effects will not cut it. In fact, it may make matters worse. For example, cigarette smokers know that smoking cigarettes causes cancer, but the majority of them still smoke because of the relaxation it induces. Cocaine causes the user to feel exhilaration and euphoria. Most cocaine users probably know that it is bad for them, but they continue to use it. Adding a small description of the positive and negative effects of the drugs will solve nothing. Drug addicts want the satisfaction that the specific drug induces, and many of them are beyond the point of caring whether it is harmful to them or not.

Vidal brings up another good point when he argues, "Every man, however, has the power (and should have the right) to kill himself if he chooses" (197). This may be true, but what if others are hurt or killed along the way? Even in Vidal's essay, this very point is brought up when he mentions that the United States is the creation of men who believed that a man has the right to do what he wants as long as it does not interfere with others. Applying this idea to illegal drug use, consider a man who is on MDMA (ecstacy). He may have every right to harm himself, but what if he begins to hallucinate? He starts to see family members with knives, and they are about to harm him. Or maybe he sees snakes that are about to attack him. The man begins to attack these hallucinations, but injures family members instead. Not only will the drug user harm himself, but others as well. Vidal's two ideas then conflict with each other. Men should have the right to do what they want, but to a certain extent.

In the middle of his essay, Vidal brings up another excellent point. The government tries to keep illegal drugs off the street, and that only makes people want drugs more. This makes sense: most people do not like being forbidden something that they enjoy, and it only makes them want it more. However, it makes no sense to blame the government when people give in to temptation. The government does what it can to make sure people know about their health. If an individual continues to use drugs, then that is his or her choice and not a result of the drug being perceived as forbidden and therefore desirable. Should we blame McDonald's and Burger King for serving food that makes us obese? No. We all know that fast food is fattening, but we consume it anyway.

Towards the end of his essay, Vidal blames the government for all the drug-related deaths because the drug trade makes money for the government as well as the Mafia. He makes an interesting point when he argues that if drugs were made legal, then the Bureau of Narcotics would likely vanish, and the Mafia would likely feel the blow as well. However, legalizing drugs would only provide quick and temporary solutions. Eventually more problems would arise, such as an increase in drug-related crimes due to the increased potential for people to experiment with drugs and make poor choices while under the influence. Other problems could include damage done to future generations because some of these drugs cause birth defects.

Although Vidal brings up excellent points throughout his essay, his overall argument is faulty. Legalizing drugs will only provide a quick fix. Eventually, all the problems that drug legalization may solve in the short term will amplify for future generations. All drugs can damage a person's health; there is no good drug out in the world. Do we really want to be responsible for that? A burden such as this one should fall on no one's head. Drugs should not be legalized.

Chapter Eleven: Using Outside Sources

Many students dread writing research papers. They're harder to write than something that you base entirely on your own thoughts or experiences. There's more work involved in finding, reading and evaluating sources. And then there's the whole process of documenting your sources and figuring out just how that's done properly.

It's true that using outside sources in your writing does add extra steps to the process, and learning to do this effectively may seem like one more huge hoop you have to jump through. However, you should also realize that this is predominately the type of writing you will be doing throughout the rest of your academic career, so you may as well start getting good at it. It will be unusual for the professors in your junior and senior years to ask you to write about personal experiences or to provide your own analysis of a book or film or current trend in a particular field. Certainly, your unique point of view will still be an important factor in your writing. However, those professors will also be looking to see how effectively you are able to blend your position with those of other experts in the field.

So, rather than fear the inevitable or shrug off this kind of writing as something you won't need in your major, you will be far better served by learning how to do it now when the demands, and possibly the stakes, aren't as high as they will be in a few years.

The Research Process

In some courses, your professors will give you specific tasks and guidelines that will steer your research and writing. Sometimes, they will be looking for you to demonstrate your ability to put the ideas of other scholars in dialogue with one another so you can show your reader the range or breadth of thinking on a particular issue. At other times, though, you will be asked to present your own views on a specific subject, using data and expert opinions to support the position you are taking. When the guidelines are specific, your job is actually a bit easier than when you are given free reign

to choose your topic and how you will approach it. In either case, the process is basically the same:

- **Do some preliminary reading**
- **Decide on a research question**
- **Start gathering sources**
- **Evaluate your sources**
- **Read and annotate your sources**
- **Draft the paper**
- **Check your documentation**

Here are a few more basic things to consider before starting:

Don't Procrastinate. Putting off any part of the research process until later (whenever that is) will lead to more problems than you can imagine. If your instructor has deadlines for the various steps in the process, make sure you meet all of them. Once you get behind, it is extremely difficult to get caught up, and the quality of your work will suffer. Try to work on your paper a little bit every day.

Use Good Organization. Choose a method for note taking (discussed later) and stick with it. Keep your notes all in one place. Keep the research material you have gathered in one place. If you download material or consult research materials in the library that cannot be checked out, make sure you accurately write down all the bibliographic information (more on this later, too) before moving on to another source. If you don't have all the information you need (or thought you already had) when the time comes to write the draft, you will waste time trying to find it, and the quality of your work will suffer.

Keep Track of Quoted Material. If you get quotations from sources you consult, make sure you put quotation marks around the authors' words and accurately record where the information came from (author, page numbers, etc.). If you're sloppy about quoting, it becomes easy later on to mistake someone else's writing for your own. This can lead to accidental plagiarism, which could be a major problem for you. Also, remember to **quote exactly** as the original material appeared in the source you're consulting.

And, Speaking of Plagiarizing, Don't Do It. Plagiarizing is copying and can take a variety of forms. Sometimes, it stems from an innocent mistake—sloppy note taking, quoting or documenting leads to a student accidentally making it seem as though he or she has written something that actually came from another writer. This can be avoided simply by being careful and accurate in your note taking. Often, though, plagiarism occurs when students "borrow" material from the Internet or other locations without giving credit or using quotation marks. Maybe they do it because the material they're using sounds impressive. When their instructors discover the plagiarism, however, they are far from impressed. Another type of plagiarism involves students "borrowing," buying or downloading whole papers or parts of papers from friends or online paper mills. Most instructors view this as a more serious offense that could lead to all sorts of problems for the student. The fact is, students usually plagiarize because they are desperate, but passing off as your own material you did not write is essentially a form of theft that instructors generally do not take kindly to. Even if you're desperate for a good grade, plagiarizing to get it will almost certainly not give you the desired results.

Preliminary Reading

More than likely, you have already done some general reading on the subject you're writing about. In most lower division classes, you are not an expert in the subject and are learning about it; the reading you do in such a class typically gives you some background and a sense of the breadth and depth of the issues. Thus, by the time you reach the point where you must begin incorporating other sources into your essays, you have probably already read some material that helps you understand where your views lie within the broader range of issues.

However, in some cases you will be asked to write a paper on a subject that you have not done much reading on, a subject that you may not know much about before beginning. Just as you had to engage in the Invention or Discovery process as part of writing other essays, so now must you also figure out what you think and what you know about your topic before you get very far into it. However, rather than brainstorming or clustering to discover some ideas, you now need to do some reading.

In this stage of the process, you should read some general background material. This is the kind of information found in encyclopedias or other general reference works. Note that at this point, you are likely not yet doing actual research for your paper. In other words, **material from encyclopedias or other general works should not be used as one of the sources in your paper**—unless your instructor requires such material, of course.

Rather, general background reading should serve to familiarize you with your subject. Don't try to read a whole book on the subject, and don't get bogged down in the small details. At this point, you're still trying to figure out what specifically you want to write about, and this background reading is supposed to help point you in that direction. As you read, look for elements of the subject that strike you as particularly interesting, the sorts of topics that seem most important or controversial, or aspects of the subject that seem especially rich with possibilities.

You are moving from looking at a broad **subject**, such as politics, and toward your **specific topic**, such as a specific policy of a particular administration, for example.

The Research Question

If you have not been assigned a specific research question, then it is time for you to develop one. Once you have focused on a topic, you should try to develop a question that your paper will explore and try to answer. When arriving at your topic and the question that you will explore, try to follow these guidelines (unless specifically instructed to do otherwise):

Make your topic narrow and focused. Students often think that broad topics will be easier to write about than narrow, specific topics. However, choosing a topic that is too broad will likely cause you to do little more than skim the surface and provide generalizations rather than digging into the topic and writing a paper that has some depth to it. A topic like politics is too broad. So is George W. Bush's presidency. However, a specific policy that grew out of his presidency—like the "No Child Left Behind" program—is much more specific and would be easier to focus on.

Choose a topic that others have written about. If you choose an obscure topic—like 14th Century Turkish pottery, for example—you will likely have a difficult time writing about it since there won't be much research you can draw upon. A topic that is more current or about which many scholars have already written will provide you with more material to draw upon.

Choose a topic you find interesting. If you've been assigned to write about a political topic, but the "No Child Left Behind" policy is of no interest to you, by all means, don't write about it. You will be bored throughout the research process, and your boredom will be evident in the paper you write. Instead, try to find a topic that fascinates you, perhaps one that angers or perplexes you. If you can possibly make the topic relate to your other interests, so much the better.

Once you have arrived at a specific topic, having a focused **research question** will help you move forward with your paper. This is more effective than trying to develop a thesis at this point in the process. Here are some examples of questions that could be used to guide research for a variety of topics:

- Will a campus-wide smoking ban be good or bad for the college?
- Should this state require people to spay and neuter their pets?
- Do drug awareness programs succeed in keeping kids from experimenting with drugs?
- Should illegal file sharing of copyrighted material be treated as a serious crime, or a sign of changes in technology that simply need to be accepted?

- What would be the benefit of letting students take general education courses credit/no credit instead of for grades?

Try to come up with a list of questions on the topic you have chosen, and then narrow the list, focusing on the question that seems most interesting to you and about which you think you could find significant material. It is not necessary at this point to have an answer to the question, and it may be better if you approach your subject without already having a specific answer. Let the question guide the research as you proceed and let your opinion on the subject grow out of what you find.

Gathering Sources

In the Dark Ages (before the Internet), student researchers actually had to go to the library to find material for their papers. With changes in technology, it is possible now for much of your research to be conducted online and in the comfort of your home. However, it is a mistake to disregard the library altogether. In fact, using your school's library as your research base will allow you to be more productive than relying on the Internet.

If you use a search engine like Google or Yahoo! to look for material on a topic like banning smoking on college campuses, you will get thousands of hits.

For example, this Google search yielded more than 46,000 hits—far too many for you to read and evaluate effectively. Many students using a search engine like this for their research will click on the first few links and then consider their research complete. The problem is that such research is limited to very few types of information. Effective research is more often based on a **variety of sources**.

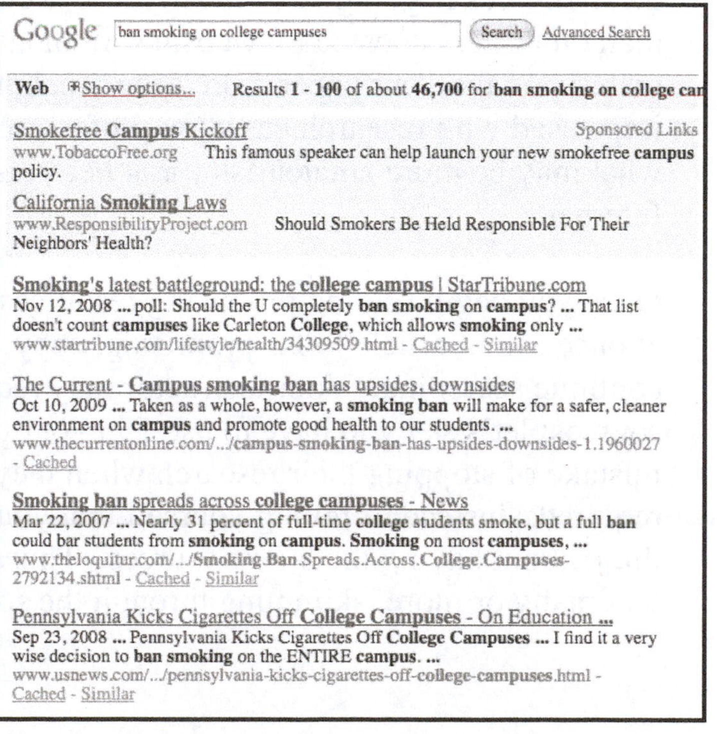

Notice that the first few items are "Sponsored Links." This means that the companies that have put together the web sites have paid to have their links come up first in searches. There may be useful information on these sites, but they also may be more biased than you would like for your research since the sponsoring organizations have a definite agenda regarding smoking. Thus, they may present the information differently than would a site designed to present the facts in a less biased way.

Rather than do a Google or Yahoo! search, you are better off consulting your library's **databases**. These are collections of materials that have already been evaluated by professionals and are likely less biased, more reliable, and more varied in the types of information they present. Most college libraries subscribe to a variety of databases, many of which are accessible from off-campus computers. Usually, you will need a password to access these databases, and when you do, you have access to thousands of sources, many of which are available in full text versions that can be downloaded to your computer or printed.

You are also far more likely to find items in a database search that come from professional journals and other scholarly sources. By making use of such sources, your paper will be based on the most current thinking on the subject. Also, since items don't appear in professional journals unless they have already been evaluated by other experts in the field, the information in these sources is going to be much more accurate and more well-respected than other items posted on websites, in blogs, etc. Not only will such material make your paper more accurate, but most instructors are far more impressed with research based on professional, scholarly sources rather than what may be more amateurish (or at best, less reliable) material found on the Internet.

Once you begin finding promising resources, you don't need to read them all at once. If an article looks promising, copy, save, download, or print it and continue searching. Your instructor may require a certain number of sources; let's say you have to use 5 in your paper. Many students make the mistake of stopping their research when they find the minimum number required. Instead of telling yourself that you need 5 sources, you should think about having the 5 *best* sources. Thus, don't stop at 5. Gather twice that many or more, skimming through the sources to see if they're relevant and appropriate to your topic. You'll read them in more detail in the next step.

Evaluating Sources

Once you have gathered several potential sources, it's time to read through the material more carefully and evaluate the authors and the texts. In the previous chapter, you learned about evaluating other writers' arguments. The things you considered then were:

- Consider the conditions under which the text was written
- Examine the author's relationship with his/her audience
- Carefully analyze the structure of the text
- Question how effectively the author presents his/her material

You should follow the same process in evaluating sources for a research paper, but you should also try to determine the **credibility** of the authors you're considering as sources. If an article was not written by an expert in the field, then it should be clear that experts were consulted. You should also look for ways that the author demonstrates that the text has been written without any unfair bias. If the original source material was peer-reviewed, that adds to the author's credibility since this means that the material could not have been published without other experts in the field evaluating the material first. Most professional journals are peer-reviewed, and you would do well to base your research on at least some material originally published in journals rather than magazines or websites.

In considering whether a source will be useful or not, you must also consider its **relevance**. Look at how recently the material was published. If you're doing a research paper about a disease like AIDS, you will want to base your research on the most recent data; material written ten years ago may be out of date and no longer relevant.

Finally, you should make sure you have a **variety** of sources. Good research papers are often based on material from different types of sources. Since there are different processes for getting material published in newspapers, magazines, journals, books, and the Internet, the types of information in those different sources will vary. Thus, a balanced and thorough research paper will not rely strictly on material from just one type of source. A paper with some information from books, journals and reputable websites will likely be more effective than one that is based strictly on material from the Internet, or strictly from books.

Once you've evaluated several potential sources and have decided on which ones to keep and which to discard, you're ready to move on to the next step. If, of course, your evaluation reveals that none of the items you've gathered so far are going to be useful, it's time to go back to the previous stage and start looking for more material. Try not to let yourself get frustrated if this happens. It's part of the process and one more reason not to save all of this work for the day or two before the first draft is due.

Reading Your Sources and Taking Notes

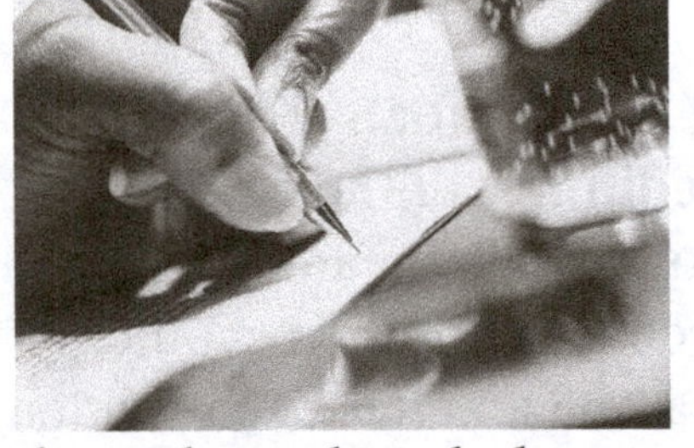

Now that you have some sources, it's time to read through them even more carefully and annotate them in preparation for using quoted, paraphrased and summarized material in your paper. As was mentioned before, it's extremely important that you are organized and accurate throughout the whole research process, but once you start taking notes on your sources, organization and accuracy become far more important to your success.

The first thing you should do (if you haven't done it already) is gather all of the **bibliographic information** on each of the sources you think you'll use.

For a **book**, you will need:

- Author
- Title
- Publisher (usually stated at the bottom of the title page)
- City of publication (usually listed below the name of the publisher. If more than one city is listed, just write down the first one. If it's a city the reader may not be familiar with, write down the city and state. In other words, if the book was published in Boston or Atlanta, you wouldn't need to write "Boston, Massachusetts" or "Atlanta, Georgia," but if the book was published in Bowling Green, Pennsylvania, then you should write down city and state.)

- Year of publication (found on the copyright page, usually right after the title page. If more than one year is listed, just write down the most recent.)

For an **article or essay that is included in an anthology**, you will need:

- Author of the article
- Title of the article
- Editor of the anthology
- Title of the anthology
- Publisher
- City of publication
- Year of publication
- Page numbers in which the article appeared

For a **hard copy of a magazine, journal or newspaper article**, you will need:

- Author of the article
- Title of the article
- Name of the magazine, journal or newspaper
- Date of publication
- Volume numbers or issue numbers (if provided)
- Page numbers on which the article appeared

For **information retrieved from the Internet** (including library databases), you will need:

- Author (if available)
- Title
- Name of sponsoring organization (such as university or publication)
- If the material is from an online magazine, journal or newspaper, you will need the name of the publication.
- Date posted or published (if available)
- Volume numbers or issue numbers (if provided)
- If the material originally appeared in hard copy format, list the page numbers of the original publication
- If you accessed the material through a database, include the name of the database.
- Date you accessed the material.

Once you've gathered all of the bibliographic information, start reading and taking notes. There are a few different methods you can use when making notes based on outside sources.

The traditional method is to use 3 x 5 note cards. To do this properly, you should have a stack of cards. Each time you come across a piece of information you think might be useful for your paper, write it down on a single card. Remember: only one piece of information per card. If you find eight items in an article, you'll use eight note cards. In the main part of the card, you should summarize or paraphrase the information you think is important (more on this later). You can also quote the material, but if you do, remember to **quote exactly word-for-word** as the information appeared in the source. Also remember to use quotation marks; otherwise, you might forget that this is a quotation and accidentally treat it as something you have written. On each card, write the author's name and the page number where you found the item you're making notes on. If there is no author, write down the title. You should also write a short heading for the material so you can go back later and quickly see what the information is about without having to read the entire card. For instance, if you're writing about music piracy, and you come across some statistics, you could simply write the word "statistics" in the upper left corner. Later, when you start drafting the paper, you can group your cards by subject as a way of helping you organize the draft.

Here is an example of how a note card ought to look. The student is reading an article by someone named Jackson, and the material is being summarized.

Justification for downloading

There are many ways people justify illegal downloads, but one of the main ones seems to be that listeners think the musicians are already rich enough and that they won't be hurt by not receiving money for one more copy of the song.

Jackson 38

An alternative to the traditional note card system is to do the same basic thing with computer files. Open a new file for each source that you use. As you read the material, type out paraphrases, summaries and quotations of material you think may be useful. For each item you type, include the page number and give a short heading. Later, you can open several files and copy and paste the material into the draft of your paper as you work on it.

Another method is to gather hard copies of all your sources and make notes directly on them. Doing this will require you to photocopy pages out of any books you plan to use or from any other hard copies of journal or magazine articles you have found in your library's reference section. It may be useful to highlight information you think you'll want to quote or to make notes in the margins around information you think you'll want to paraphrase or summarize.

Regardless of the method you choose for note taking, it is important that you stay organized. Once you have a method you feel comfortable with, stick with it, and keep all of your notes in one place.

Take your time reading and taking notes. Again, this is a process that will not go smoothly if you procrastinate. Once you've read your sources, taken good notes on them, and are reasonably sure you have enough material to base your paper on, it's time to start drafting.

Drafting the Research Paper

For the most part, drafting a research paper is not much different than drafting any other essay. You need a basic working thesis and a rough outline. You'll need to give some thought to how you should organize your paper and the tone you want to take. And, of course, you'll need to keep in mind the requirements of the assignment; no matter how brilliant your paper may be, if it doesn't demonstrate things your instructor expects to see, it's not likely that the paper will be as successful as you'd hoped.

However, there are definitely some things that make research-based writing different from essays that are based strictly on personal experience, thoughts or observations. Now, you're trying to combine your ideas with those of experts in the field. You may be using your research to show that your views are in keeping with what others believe. You may be using your research to show that there are differences of opinion among experts and how your position blends with others'. You may be using your research to give your reader background information and a sense of perspective on your topic. Of course, you could also be doing several of these things, or something else altogether.

Here's what you **don't** want to do, though: You don't want your paper simply to report on what other people think. There may, of course, be times when an instructor asks you to do exactly that; if so, by all means follow instructions. Most often, though, instructors assign research papers so that students can **synthesize** their views with the views held by other writers; that is, your goal is to blend your views with those of the people you've been reading. Just listing what different experts have said on your topic leaves out the most important element: your own point of view.

When working with material drawn from your sources, you need to decide if you are going to **quote, paraphrase** or **summarize** what other authors have written. You've already read about quoting in Chapter Nine and should look at that section again to refresh your memory. Here are the basic principles to consider, though, when quoting.

- Choose quotations that are vivid and interesting, phrased in a way that you could not improve on.
- Quote exactly, word-for-word as the language appeared in the original source.
- Introduce quotations with an acknowledging phrase, such as "Jane Smith writes…" or "Bob Blank has argued…"
- Don't use **freestanding quotations** (that is, quotations without an introductory or acknowledging phrase).

Additionally, you may find that something in the quotation needs to be changed or modified in order for it to make sense for your reader. Even though you must quote word-for-word, it is possible to make minor changes for clarity's sake as long as you format these changes correctly. The example from Jack London in Chapter Nine reads, in part,

> "Treat John Barleycorn the same way. Stop him. Don't let him lie around, licensed and legal, to pounce upon our youth."

Let's say it's not necessary for you to use the phrase "John Barleycorn" to mean alcohol; the phrase may do nothing to add to your argument, and you don't want to have to explain it for your reader. So, it would be acceptable to quote London this way:

> "Treat [alcohol] the same way. Stop [it]. Don't let [it] lie around, licensed and legal, to pounce upon our youth."

Here the brackets [ ] indicate that something has been added or changed in the quoted material. As long as the bracketed material does not change the meaning of the original quotation, it is acceptable to do this.

Similarly, you may find that there is material within a quotation that does not suit your needs. In this case, it is acceptable to delete a part of a quotation as long as the deletion does not change the meaning and as long as you clearly indicate for your reader that something has been removed. For instance, in the above example, let's say you want to leave the "John Barleycorn" reference, but you don't want the short sentence "Stop it" since you feel it is repetitive. In this case, you could quote London this way:

> "Treat John Barleycorn the same way. […] Don't let him lie around, licensed and legal, to pounce upon our youth."

Here, the brackets with the ellipsis in them […] indicates that something has been removed from the original.

One other rule about quotations: if the quotation takes up four lines or more when you type it into your paper, you need to format it as a **block quotation**. In a block quotation, you indent the entire quotation five spaces, and you do not use quotation marks. The following is taken from a student paper on the film *American History X*, which suggests that racism is taught rather than naturally occurring. The student agrees with the film's message and uses an example from Frederick Douglass' *Narrative of the Life of Frederick Douglass, an American Slave* to add to his analysis.

> While the filmmakers show that racism can be taught through the fictional characters they have created, the film's point clearly holds true in real life settings as well. In *Narrative of the Life of Frederick Douglass, an American Slave*, the author recalls the slave mistress he knew as a child and the effects that slavery had on her. A northerner who had married a southern plantation owner, the mistress started out kind and not thinking of the slaves as things her husband owned. However, as Douglass writes,
>
>> Slavery proved as injurious to her as it did to me. When I went there, she was a pious, warm, and tender-hearted woman. There was no sorrow or suffering for which she had not a tear. She had bread for the hungry, clothes for the naked, and comfort for every mourner that came within her reach. Slavery soon proved its ability to divest her of these heavenly qualities. Under its influence, the tender heart became stone, and the lamblike disposition gave way to one of tiger-like fierceness.
>
> In this way, Douglass shows his readers that a woman who had once been good and kind and thought of slaves as people to be treated tenderly soon was transformed into a cruel mistress. This did not occur naturally, but had to be taught by her husband.

Notice that the student used an acknowledging phrase to transition into the quotation. Again, there are no quotation marks, and the entire block quotation is indented. Also note that the student continues the paragraph after the quotation is completed. Oftentimes, students will set their word processors to indent automatically after they hit the "enter" key, making it look as though what follows the quotation is a new paragraph. If you don't intend to start a new paragraph, then make sure you're not indenting.

Most writing instructors would agree that it is best when students quote sparingly. Too many students give in to the temptation to quote often and to use lengthy quotations. A good rule to follow would be to quote no more than once per page and to use only one block quotation in a whole paper. Even this may be too much quoting, however, and it may be best to ask your instructor for any specific guidelines. Again, you should quote only when the original phrasing is perfect to your purpose. Most often, you can put the information from your source into your own words either through a **paraphrase** or **summary**.

You studied summary writing in Chapter Nine as well and should review that section again. For now, remember that a summary captures the main ideas of the material you are writing, not the little details. Summaries should always be shorter than the original material.

A paraphrase, however, is something different. When you paraphrase, you are putting a specific piece of information into your own words. This is more challenging than it may sound and requires some practice. Many students are under the impression that in order to paraphrase correctly, all they need to do is change one or two words in the original source material. This is, in fact, plagiarism and should be avoided. Instead, properly paraphrased material communicates the facts and ideas found in the original but does so entirely in the student's own words. Granted, there may be a few words in the paraphrase that also appeared in the original, but the tone, style and sentence structure should all be the student's.

For example, consider the Pledge of Allegiance: "I pledge allegiance to the flag of the United States of America, and to the republic for which it stands, one nation under God, indivisible, with liberty and justice for all."

An improper paraphrase might look like this:

> "I promise allegiance to the American flag and to the country for which it stands, one country that is under God and indivisible and in which everyone can find liberty and justice."

While some of the language has changed—*promise* instead of *pledge*, *American flag* instead of *flag of the United States of America*, etc.—there is far too much in the paraphrase that is exactly the same as the original. Furthermore, the structure of the paraphrase mirrors the original exactly. This is the kind of attempt at paraphrasing that happens when a student writer has the original passage in front of him or her and tries to write a new version while looking at the original. Trying to do so makes sense since the student doesn't want to leave out anything important, but the result is not satisfactory.

Instead, an effective paraphrase can be written when you follow these steps:

- Read the original passage several times, not to memorize it, but to understand it and make sure you know the most important information.
- Set the original aside; close the book or minimize the web page. Don't have it visible.
- Still without looking at the original, try to write your own version, getting the facts into the paraphrase but not worrying about the original phrasing.
- Compare your paraphrase with the original. If any phrases are too close to the original, find another way to say what you want. If any important information has been left out of the paraphrase, find a way to work it in.

Here is a better paraphrase of the Pledge of Allegiance:

> "The American flag is a symbol of a country that values individual freedom and strives to treat all of its people fairly. Founded on religious principles, it is a country that cannot be divided, and I swear that I will be true to the flag and everything it represents."

Notice that the paraphrase is longer than the original. This is typical. The main thing to remember when paraphrasing is that the new version must capture the meaning of the original phrase without using the other authors' phrasing. This is not easy and requires some practice. If you rush this process when drafting your paper, the result will likely not be as strong as you would like.

Your Turn

Find a short passage (no more than 2 or 3 sentences) in any text that you would like to practice with. Read the passage several times, trying to remember the basic information. Then put the text away. On a separate sheet of paper, write a paraphrase, focusing on including as much of the information from the original as possible. When you are finished, compare your paraphrase with the original. If any phrases are too close to the original, change them, and if any important information has been left out, add it.

There is one other key difference between drafting an essay using outside sources and one that doesn't. When working with material drawn from research, you must properly document your sources, and it is far easier to incorporate documentation **as you draft the paper** rather than trying to go back later and add documentation to an already completed draft. Because of this, make sure you read the following section before beginning your draft.

Documentation

This may be the element of research-based writing that most intimidates students since there are a lot of rules to remember, and it's easy to make mistakes. However, if you follow the steps explained in this section, you shouldn't have a problem. Many students make the mistake of assuming they must memorize the format for documentation when in fact most instructors would not expect that of their students. In writing with sources for this class, you are demonstrating an ability to work with other authors' ideas and to give credit to your sources. If you treat this book as a resource to help you do that, you should be fine. If you read it once and then try to document your sources without consulting the book again, it's not likely to go well.

The first step in properly documenting a research paper is to put together a **Works Cited** list. This will eventually be the last page of your completed paper. Note that this is not the same thing as a bibliography. What's the difference? A bibliography is a list of everything that has been written on a subject, or it can also be a list of every source that you consulted in putting your paper together. However, if you only read a source and didn't actually cite it in the paper (more on citing in a bit), then it would not appear in the Works Cited list. Instead, only the sources you actually cite go in this list.

Remember the bibliographic information you gathered when deciding on which sources you should use? Now it's time to get those notes out and start arranging the information in a uniform order.

Note: Some academic libraries subscribe to services that will format your works cited list for you. Other such services are available online, many of them at no cost to users. All you need to do is input the proper information. Find out if your instructor has any policy regarding the use of such resources before using them. Even if you are using such a resource, however, it is still important for you to understand how a works cited list ought to be formatted in order for you to be sure that you are inputting the correct information.

Following are the most common types of sources used in papers at this academic level, arranged in MLA format. This is the most common type of formatting used in English classes. If your instructor has asked you to use a different format, such as APA or Chicago style, make sure you look it up and follow those directions instead. For MLA format, find the type of source that matches the one you're working with and use the example as a model to format the bibliographic information you have. If you're using a source not listed below, ask your instructor for assistance. More examples can usually be found on the Internet or at your college library.

In MLA format, you must provide your reader with in-text citations. That is, when you make reference to a source in your paper, you will either mention the author's name as part of your acknowledging phrase or else in parentheses right after the quotation, summary or paraphrase. If the source is electronic or doesn't have page numbers, then you only need to mention the author's name. If no author is named, you will use the title to reference the source. Examples of how to cite sources in your paper come immediately after the examples showing how to format the works cited entries.

Books

Here is the basic bibliographic format for a book:

> Author's Last Name, Author's First Name. *Title*. City of Publication: Publisher, Year of Publication. Print.

Following are some specific examples. Notice the particular type of book and author you are working with, and format your entry the same way.

A book with one author:

Kerouac, Jack. *On the Road.* New York: Viking, 1957. Print.

To cite this source, use the author's last name and page number: (Kerouac 68)

A book with two authors:

Morella, Joe, and Edward Z. Epstein. *The "It" Girl: The Incredible Story of Clara Bow.* New York: Delacorte, 1976. Print.

Citation: (Morella and Epstein 93)

A book with more than three authors:

Davidson, James West, et. al. *Nation of Nations: A Narrative History of the American Republic.* Boston: McGraw, 2008. Print.

Citation: (Davidson 112)

An article or essay appearing in an anthology, or collection of essays:

For this type of source, you will need the author of the article, the title of the article, the name of the anthology, the editor of the anthology, the rest of the publication information for the book, and the page numbers that the essay appeared on. **Note that you are citing the author of the article or essay, not the editor of the whole book.**

Example:

Bronson, Fred. "A Selected Chronology of Musical Controversy." *Reading and Writing Short Arguments*. Ed. William Vesterman. New York: McGraw-Hill, 2006. 257-62. Print.

Citation: (Bronson 258)

Periodicals

Here is the basic bibliographic format for a print edition of a newspaper, magazine, or journal:

Author's Last Name, First Name. "Title of Article." *Title of Periodical* Day Month Year: Pages. Print.

Following are some specific examples. Note the type of periodical you are working with and format your entry the same way.

An article in a magazine:

Herper, Matthew. "Cancer Man." *Forbes* 19 Oct. 2009: 154-156. Print.

Citation: (Herper 155)

An article in a newspaper:

Lee, Don. "Jobs Scarce for New Grads." *Los Angeles Times* 14 Dec. 2009: A1. Print.

If an article is only one page long, you do not need to list the page number in your citation:

Citation: (Lee)

For an anonymous article, start with the title and then provide the rest of the information as you normally would:

"The Cost of Dropping Out." *Neatoday* Jan./Feb. 2010: 18. Print.

Remember to cite the title of the unsigned article, or the first few words of a longer title, **not** the name of the periodical.

Citation: ("The Cost of Dropping Out")

Articles in scholarly journals:

The format is slightly different for journals, since they are usually identified by volume and issue number rather than day, month, and year. Here is the basic format:

> Last Name, First Name. "Title of Article." *Journal Name* Volume.Issue (year): pages. Print.

For example:

> Wyrick, Laura. "Summoning Candyman." *Arizona Quarterly* 54.3 (1998): 89-117. Print.

> Citation: (Wyrick 93)

Electronic Sources

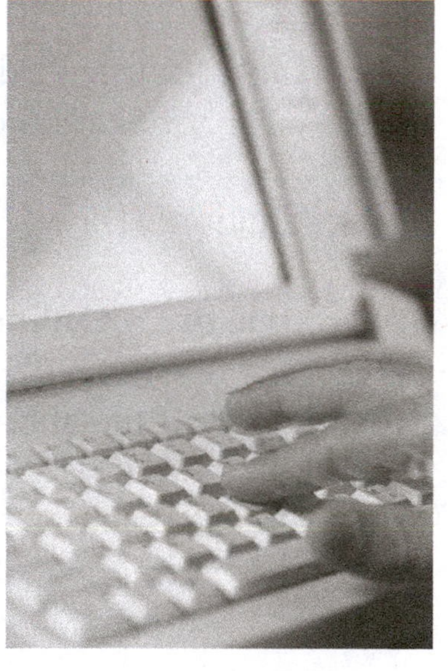

Given the opportunity, most student writers seem to prefer working with electronic rather than print sources. There is nothing wrong with this; however, you need to be much more careful about evaluating sources found online to make sure they are accurate and free of biases that might weaken your paper if you site such sources. As mentioned earlier, you are better off using sources found through a database like Ebscohost, Proquest, etc. rather than relying on Google or Yahoo! searches. Be especially careful of sites like wikipedia that rely on users to upload content; many professors will not consider material from such sites to be reliable or appropriate for academic writing.

The basic format for citing electronic sources is as follows:

> Author or editor (when available). "Title of article." *Name of website.* Version number (if available). Name of sponsoring organization, date posted. Medium of publication. Date you accessed the material.

Keep in mind that you will not always have all of the information listed above or in the following examples. The most important thing is that you follow the format as closely as possible, using all the bibliographic information that you **do** have in order to allow your reader to find the same material easily.

NOTE: If a website does not include information on when the material in it was posted or created, use the abbreviation n.d. (no date).

Following are some examples. Note the type of source you are working with and format your entries accordingly.

A Page on a Website:

"Imagining College Without Grades." *Insidehighered.com.* Inside Higher Ed, 22 Jan. 2009. Web. 20 Jan. 2010.

Citation: ("Imagining")

Davy, Laura. "Alternatives to a Traditional College." *Education.com.* Education.com., n.d. Web. 22 Jan. 2010.

Citation: (Davy)

An Article in an Online Scholarly Journal:

Note the use of the abbreviation n.pag. for "no page."

Dreier, Peter, and John Atlas. "*The Wire*—Bush-Era Fable about America's Urban Poor?" *City and Community* 8.3 (2009): n.pag. Web. 13 Jan. 2010.

Citation: (Dreier and Atlas)

An Article Retrieved from an Online Database:

In citing such material, it is important that you include the name of the database you used to access the material. Italicize the name of the database. Common databases include JSTOR, Ebscohost, ProQuest, and CQ

Researcher; your library may use others. Otherwise, follow the same format that you would for print versions of the same types of sources—that is, magazine, journal, newspaper, etc.

> Seo, Dong-Chul, and Nan Jiang. "Associations between Smoking and Extreme Dieting among Adolescents." *Journal of Youth and Adolescence*, 38.10 (2009): 1364-1373. *Ebscohost*. Web. 20 Jan. 2010.

When citing this source, you would not refer to page numbers even though the print version's page numbers are included. When reading the electronic version, you have no way of knowing how it corresponds to the page numbers in the printed version. Thus, your citation would look like this:

> (Seo and Jiang)

Your Turn

All of the bibliographic information for the following resources has been scrambled. For each item, consult the examples in the previous pages and rewrite the information in the proper format. Remember to indent properly.

An article from a newspaper: The article appeared in The Los Angeles Times on page B3 on October 19, 2008. The title is "New Machines for Old" and the author is Jason Trumble. The article was read in a print version.

A book: The publisher is Roxbury Press, which is located in New York. The author is Eileen Jenkins. The book was published in 2006. The title is When We Can't Get Along. The book was read in a print version.

An unsigned article in a magazine: The magazine is Runners Monthly, and the article appeared in the September 2007 issue on pages 64-71. The title of the article is "Runners' High, Runners' Low." The article was read in a print version.

An article from a website: The sponsoring organization is NPR, and its website is npr.org. The article was posted on January 20, 2010 and was accessed on Februay 15, 2010. Its title is "GOP Win Unlikely To Derail Obama's Entire Agenda." The article was read online.

An essay in an anthology: The essay's title is "Ridley Scott and Philip K. Dick" and it appears on pages 278-283 of a book called On Philip K. Dick: 40 Articles from *Science Fiction Studies*. The author of the essay is Jake Jakaitis. The book was published by SF-TH, which is located in Terre Haute, Indiana. The book's editor is R.D. Mullen, and it was published in 1992. The article was read in a print version.

An article retrieved from an online database: The author is Sharon Gaudin. The article appeared in the February 2010 issue of a magazine called Macworld on page 70. The article was retrieved through the Academic Search Premiere database. Its title is "Business Use of Twitter, Facebook Exploding." It was accessed on March 18, 2010.

A Sample Research Paper

Here is a prompt for a research paper:

Writing Assignment: Using Other Writers' Ideas

In preparation for writing this paper, you should read these three resources:

Manzo, Kathleen Kennedy. "Twitter Lessons in 140 Characters or Less." *Education Week* 29.8 (2009): 1-14. *Academic Search Premier*. Web. 10 May 2010.

Miners, Zach. "Twitter Takes a Trip to College." *U.S. News & World Report* Sep. 2009: 56-57. *Academic Search Premier*. Web. 10 May 2010.

Young, Jeffrey R. "Teaching With Twitter: Not for the Faint of Heart." *Chronicle of Higher Education* 56.14 (2009): A1-A11. *Academic Search Premier*. Web. 10 May 2010.

All are available online; remember that when you cite these sources, you should include the dates when **you** accessed them, not the dates provided here.

Once you have read and thought about these articles, taking good notes along the way, you need to formulate your own position on the use of social networking websites like Twitter in academic settings.

Do you feel it is a good idea or not? Be sure to explain your position in clear, logical terms, letting your reader know what facts you base your views on. Make sure you use specific, detailed examples drawn from the sources provided and possibly from your own observations and experiences.

All sources must be properly documented in MLA format. To receive a minimum passing score on this assignment, you must:

- Quote effectively from at least two of the sources.
- Paraphrase or summarize material from all three sources.
- Smoothly integrate the material drawn from the sources into your own writing.

Your final draft should be 4-5 pages, typed and double-spaced.

After following all of the steps outlined in this chapter, a student wrote the essay found on the following pages. As you read, take note of the ways the student weaves together the ideas from the source material with her own views. You should also pay attention to MLA formatting and ask your instructor about any formatting choices that seem unclear to you.

Heading is properly formatted with student's name, professor, course and date all on double-spaced lines. Student's last name and page number appear in the header at the top right margin.

Title is double-spaced with no other special formatting.

Introduction begins with an attention-grabber, followed by general information to provide the reader with some background.

Thesis responds directly to the writing prompt by providing the student's position—which the rest of the paper will support.

Talbot 1

Jennifer Talbot

Professor Haines

English 100

15 December 2009

If You Can't Beat 'Em, Join 'Em:

Twitter Goes to College

The professor turns her back on the class, and her students' thumbs immediately begin to fly across the keys on their cell phones. They are not, however, breaking the rules or doing anything that their professor would disapprove of. Instead, the students are engaged in a new type of classroom practice. Across the country, high school and college instructors have begun using Twitter as part of their teaching strategies to make their classes more interactive and to tap into their students' interest in using technology to communicate. While some critics feel that it is improper and ineffective to invite students to text during class, the fact is that technology is changing society in countless ways. Just as the business world and the entertainment industry have adapted to these changes, the academic world must also evolve; using Twitter and other social networking services to help students engage with their classes and professors is not just a sign of the times but a valuable leap forward in education.

Twitter.com is a website that has gotten a lot of press in the last couple of years, most of it negative. Users of the site have followers subscribe to their accounts and then communicate with their followers through short messages (called *tweets*) of no more than 140

This paragraph provides general background information for readers not familiar with Twitter. Because the information is general and could be found in a variety of places with little variation, it is considered "common knowledge" and does not need to be cited.

Talbot 2

characters that are posted to the internet or delivered to their followers' cell phones as instant messages. Comedians joke about self-centered celebrities using cites like Twitter to get more people to pay attention to them, and news commentators point to politicians disrespectfully sending tweets while Congress is in session. The website's critics see it as one more way that technology makes society shallower, allowing anyone to think that his or her thoughts are so important that others will want to read them.

Paraphrased information is properly cited.

However, the site does more than just allow fans to find out what Britney Spears is ordering at Starbucks. Business professionals use Twitter to network with each other, and educators have set up Twitter accounts to share information on effective teaching practices. One popular user of the service is a Georgia teacher who has thousands of followers reading her advice on successful and innovative teaching strategies (Manzo). Recently, high school and college instructors have begun setting up Twitter accounts for their classes, and students are encouraged to send questions and comments through the site that the rest of the class and the teacher can access immediately (Manzo; Miners; Young). The question is: does this use of technology actually help students learn, or is it just a gimmick that causes more problems for students who already tend to be more comfortable with their gadgets than their books?

Summarized information from multiple sources is properly cited.

Some problems that have developed as these practices are put into use include students using Twitter during

Opposing view, followed by brief transition ("However") and the author's refutation.

Properly cited quotation with brief acknowledging phrase preceding it and short analysis of the quotation following it.

quizzes to try to get answers from fellow students, arguments developing between students through their posts to the class account, and lectures being derailed as the tweets take the class in directions the professor had not intended (Young). However, these sorts of things happen in classes all the time whether instructors are using new technology or not. Other things that typically happen in the classroom, however, can be made better with options like Twitter.

For instance, shy or quiet students who would not normally ask questions in class often feel the freedom to do so once the class has a Twitter account. One such student commented, "I'm not that outspoken in class, so I would never ask a question out loud to the professor. But you can type it in as anonymous, so nobody really knows if what you're asking is a dumb question" (Young). While some might argue that such a student needs to get over his anxiety and that his use of Twitter is just a crutch that enables him to continue being shy, the fact that he has found a way to share his thoughts with his classmates adds to the classroom experience of others, regardless of the method he uses. The same student's professor notes that since the class's Twitter account encourages more diverse responses than in a traditional class, it has led to questions and discussions that have never come up before in his long experience teaching the same subject (Young).

Other critics of Twitter suggest that the 140-character limitation on tweets prevents students from effectively expressing themselves and may actually make

More opposing views, briefly summarized. Note that all paraphrased material is cited.

Talbot 4

them less literate (Miner). Furthermore, studies have shown that the multi-tasking Twitter requires of students actually makes them less productive since doing more than one thing at a time actually results in none of the tasks being done as well as when people are able to focus on a single thing (Manzo). Finally, some urge that Twitter and other social networking services are just too new for us to really understand if they will ultimately be helpful or harmful (Manzo).

The writer acknowledges the strength of the opposition, but balances this with other factors not accounted for by opposing views.

All of these may be legitimate concerns. However, there is another fact that cannot be ignored. The Internet is developing in ways that could not have been imagined even five years ago with cites like Wikipedia, Facebook and MySpace allowing individual users to create the content of the web. Additionally, once content has been created, it remains active, being commented on and added to by other users. The Internet thus becomes something more organic than it has previously been; it is no longer just a source of information and entertainment. Instead, it becomes a form of individual and community expression, a source of creativity and growth rather than just a way to access more traditional creativity as it had previously been. According to Pamela B. Rutledge, who runs Fielding Graduate University's Media Psychology Research Center, "Today's students [...] are going to need to have highly developed critical-thinking skills, be able to digest large amounts of information, and determine what's important and what's not." Rutledge sees cites like Twitter providing students with methods to gain such skills (Manzo).

Ellipsis enclosed in brackets shows that something has been omitted from the quotation.

In the final paragraphs, the student provides her own views on the subject, based on some general examples that seem based on personal experience.

Talbot 5

The academic world needs to recognize the value of Twitter, and the few professors using the technology should be looked at as pioneers. It is true that some students are not mature enough to be able to handle the technology, but there are immature students in almost every class. These are the ones who used to pass notes or disrupt class with jokes or noises. Today, they may text during class or send inappropriate tweets. Whether one is a professor or another student, dealing with such disruptions is just part of the college experience. For students who are more academic, though, the technology is there for us to learn from and to learn with. If we are challenged to express ourselves in 140 characters or less, we are not limited or made less literate, but must think carefully about how to get our points across.

Clear, effective conclusion.

When technology is used effectively in the classroom, students learn not only from their professors, but also from each other. Sometimes, our teachers even learn from us. People who argue that education needs to be reformed in order to keep today's students more involved have urged that professors move away from their traditional role of "sage on the stage" and toward the more interactive role of "guide on the side" (Young). While it is true that Twitter and similar technologies are new and that we may not yet know what their long-range effects on education will be (Manzo), it seems reasonable that anything that engages students in new and exciting ways and makes the exchange of ideas between students and professors easier is something that should be embraced. The future is now. Tweet on!

Works cited listed on separate page. All resources actually cited in the paper are listed alphabetically by authors' last names. Note the use of hanging indents for each entry, making it easier for readers to focus on the authors' last names, which are the terms used in parenthetical citations in the paper. All required information is present and arranged in proper MLA format.

Talbot 6

Works Cited

Manzo, Kathleen Kennedy. "Twitter Lessons in 140 Characters or Less." *Education Week* 29.8 (2009): 1-14. *Academic Search Premier*. Web. 15 May 2010.

Miners, Zach. "Twitter Takes a Trip to College." *U.S. News & World Report* Sep. 2009: 56-57. *Academic Search Premier*. Web. 15 May 2010.

Young, Jeffrey R. "Teaching With Twitter: Not for the Faint of Heart." *Chronicle of Higher Education* 56.14 (2009): A1-A11. *Academic Search Premier*. Web. 15 May 2010.

Chapter Twelve: Writing In-Class Essays

You've been in class for several weeks and have gotten quite comfortable with the routine and the professor, but then the day comes when the professor doesn't start class in the normal way. Everyone is nervous, and you glance around to see your classmates reading their notes and hurriedly gathering pens, pencils, erasers and dictionaries. It's midterm day, and you have to spend the next hour or two writing an essay in class. When it's over, you'll hand your efforts over to your professor and hope for the best, and whether you've done well or not, you're relieved that the test is finished.

Writing an in-class essay, however, doesn't have to fill you with anxiety. The suggestions in this chapter will help you overcome those negative feelings that may come up when you know you need to perform for the professor.

Let's Break It Down

When you think about it, writing in a timed situation isn't that much different than writing one of your major papers for this class:

- You have a specific writing assignment
- The professor expects you to demonstrate your knowledge of the subject
- You need to write an essay that has a thesis, body paragraphs with specific examples that support the thesis, and a conclusion
- The essay needs to be reasonably free of grammatical errors.

The only real difference now is that you're writing this essay in one or two hours instead of one or two weeks.

Before you let that difference make you panic, though, you should realize that your professor is quite likely viewing the writing you produce during the exam differently than what you produce in your bigger papers. In other words, in an out-of-class essay, you need to demonstrate your ability to develop your thesis and support it effectively with strong, lively examples. In an in-class essay, however, you are probably expected to demonstrate different things. These could include:

- Your ability to come up with a topic and examples quickly and to organize them in a clear fashion.
- Your ability to explain important concepts that you have studied in and out of class, showing that you understand the material thoroughly.
- Your ability to analyze, explain, or argue a subject you may or may not be familiar with.

Certainly, there could be other tasks at the heart of your exam, and it's important that you understand what is expected of you going into the situation.

Regardless of the specific requirements of the assignment, there are three things to focus on that will help you do well in an in-class writing situation:

- **Being Prepared**
- **Knowing Your Strengths and Weaknesses**
- **Managing Your Time Wisely**

Just as with other elements of writing we've looked at so far, none of these aspects of in-class writing can work in isolation or by magic. If you've struggled with in-class writing before, just reading this chapter won't work miracles for you. Instead, you need to work at this, perhaps even writing some practice essays to help get yourself ready. As with everything else you've done so far, this skill needs to be worked at in order for you to improve.

Being Prepared

This is probably the single most important thing you can do to help you do well in an in-class essay. If you've had problems with test anxiety in the past, coming into an exam situation as fully prepared as possible can help you avoid this problem, and all the other problems that go with it. Here's what you can do to help yourself:

Know the Material. If your instructor is giving you an essay exam based on material you're supposed to have studied, then make sure you've studied it. If it's a text you were supposed to read, then make sure you budget enough time to read and understand it. Annotate the text, study your notes,

and see your professor if there's anything about the text that confuses you. If the instructor's goal is to have you demonstrate your understanding of the material, you won't be able to do that without at least giving yourself plenty of time to read and study. If it's a particular skill your instructor needs you to demonstrate—such as writing an argument or a description—then make sure you understand how that's done. Study the sections of your text that show how that skill should be performed, and practice if possible before the exam.

Additionally, if your instructor has provided a study guide or allows you to bring in notes, quotations, an outline, or any other materials, take advantage of those things. Make sure you have everything you need before the writing exam is scheduled. As with every other aspect of writing well, procrastination at this stage will almost certainly work against you.

Other ways to be prepared may seem rather basic, but pay attention to them regardless. These include:

- Getting plenty of sleep
- Eating right (you don't want to have a sugar crash during the exam)
- Bringing everything you need on the day of the exam (pens, pencils, paper, a dictionary if it's allowed, etc.)

On the day of the in-class essay, try to get to class early so you have time to look over your notes and gather your materials together without being rushed. Take a few deep breaths before you start to write. If you burst into class ten minutes into the exam and have to get paper and pens from your classmates, it won't help with any anxiety you may be feeling, and it certainly won't help your classmates either!

Knowing Your Strengths and Weaknesses

By the time you're in an in-class writing situation, you likely have spent some time in the course and have had your writing evaluated. As part of your preparation for the writing exam, it's a good idea to look back over your papers—especially other things you've written in class. Study your instructor's notes and suggestions, focusing on things that seem to cause problems for you in assignment after assignment.

If it's grammar, make note of the specific problems you encounter. Look up the proper way to correct those issues (consult the grammar section at the end of this book) and work on some exercises to help give yourself a better sense of how to write correctly.

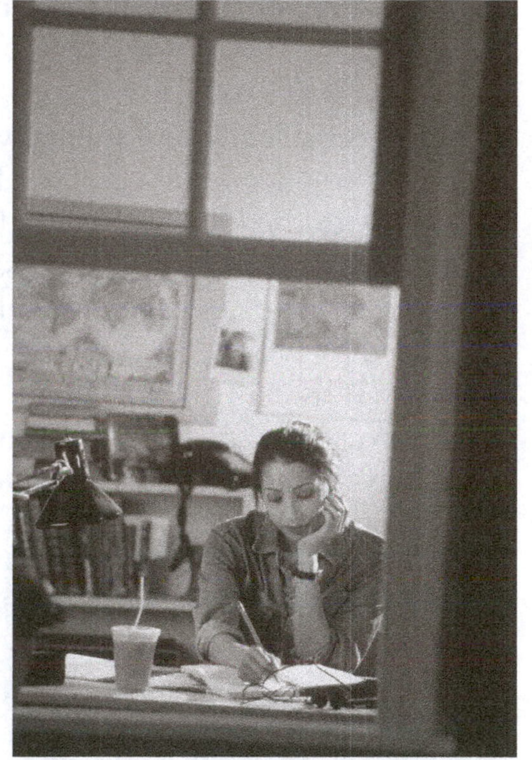

If it's organization or thesis statements or using examples that are too vague, take the time to re-write some of those older pieces. Doing so may not do anything for your past grades, but it will help you get a sense of what you should have done differently and what you can avoid in future assignments—like the in-class essay that's coming up.

If you've had a problem with following directions or meeting basic requirements in an assignment, that may be something you should talk over with your instructor. At any rate, though, knowing you've had this problem should tell you that you need to spend a few extra minutes looking at the instructions and requirements once you get the essay exam. Make sure you ask for clarification from your instructor if you're not sure what's expected of you.

Of course, it's not all negative. Looking at past papers can show you the elements of writing that you've already done well with. Knowing that you have certain strengths—that you're good at using metaphors in descriptive passages, for example, or that your introductions are always lively and interesting—should increase your confidence and, again, help you prepare for the exam. If you know you already do something well, you don't need to spend as much time studying it beforehand and can devote more of your time to your trouble spots.

Managing Your Time

It is extremely important that you know how much time you are allotted for the essay you will write in class. Your instructor will likely let you know ahead of time, but if not, it's a good idea to ask.

When you write your essay, keep in mind that what you do in this exam situation is basically a shortened version of the larger writing process you used in your out-of-class essays. In those situations, you engaged in discovery, drafted your essay, and then revised and proofread. While you won't have time in an in-class essay to revise as thoroughly as you would in a longer out-of-class paper, the other steps in the process should still be employed.

This is especially true of the discovery/invention phase. If you try to write an in-class essay without giving yourself the chance to figure out what you think beforehand, you run the risk of getting off to a bad start, perhaps writing an essay that fails to address the writing prompt. Instead, take a few minutes to brainstorm, cluster, freewrite, or a combination of techniques to give yourself a chance to test your ideas before actually starting to compose your draft.

If you've paid attention to the previous section and are aware of your strengths and weaknesses, this can help you decide before even getting to class how much time you should spend on discovery/invention. For instance, if you've had trouble with organization, thesis statements or developing adequate examples in past papers, you should give yourself extra time for prewriting. Try to arrive at a rough outline and evaluate it briefly to make sure it will address the prompt.

On the other hand, if you know that organization and development are among your strengths, you may not need to spend as much time on discovery/invention and can instead devote more time to other tasks.

In the same way, if you know you struggle with elements of grammar, you should budget plenty of time for proofreading and checking your grammar. Furthermore, knowing ahead of time that this is one of your weaknesses, you should have studied the particular grammar areas that normally give you trouble. Now, you can give proper attention to these trouble spots.

Here are a couple of ways students might manage their time in an in-class writing situation. Let's say you will have 90 minutes to plan, write and proofread your essay. Student 1 has problems with grammar, Student 2 struggles with thesis statements, and Student 3 has no problems with grammar, but often writes paragraphs that are underdeveloped. Knowing their strengths and weaknesses and managing their time, these students might come up with the following strategies:

	Student 1	Student 2	Student 3
Discovery	10 minutes	15 minutes	10 minutes
Drafting	55 minutes	60 minutes	70 minutes
Proofreading	25 minutes	15 minutes	10 minutes

These are just guidelines, of course, and in reality a student with one of these plans might find that he or she needs to vary from it once the essay exam is actually underway. However, simply having a plan and breaking the allotted time into useful chunks will help such a student do well on the exam.

Your Turn

1. Take a few moments to assess your strengths and weaknesses as a writer. What do you see as your trouble spots, the things your professor has identified as aspects of your writing that need improvement? What do you think you do well?

2. Now consider the three categories above—Discovery, Drafting, and Proofreading. Given your strengths and weaknesses, which of these three areas will you need to focus on the most in order to do well on the in-class essay? Which of these three can you confidently give less time to?

3. Finally, try to find out how long you will have for the in-class essay. Considering what you have determined in steps 1 and 2 above, divide the allotted time according to your strengths and weaknesses, determining how much time you should spend on Discovery, Drafting, and Proofreading. Do this before you walk into class on the day of the exam.

Keep These Things in Mind

Here are a few more things to consider as you prepare for an in-class essay:

Don't Attempt a Rough Draft and Revision. Many students think they will have time to do a very messy rough draft followed by a neatly written revision, and they're almost always wrong. Unless you work extremely fast, you will likely run out of time and will end up needing to give your professor a couple of neatly written pages along with the scribbled version that you spent most of class on. Instead of doing it this way, stick with the writing process and let the prewriting/discovery/invention phase work for you. Let that be the messy draft that no one needs to see. When you actually start writing the essay, tell yourself this is what you will turn in for a grade. If you make mistakes, correct them along the way, but don't try to rewrite the whole thing.

Use All of the Allotted Time. If your professor gives you an hour, or an hour and a half, or even more time to write your essay, it's a good idea to use all of that time. Don't tell yourself that if you finish early, you will have time to get coffee or a nap before your next class. Part of your grade is riding on this essay, so don't sell yourself short. Budget your time, and use it wisely.

Bring Everything You Will Need to the Exam. Along with pens, pencils and paper, you may want to bring a dictionary or thesaurus (if your professor allows use of these things during the exam). You may also want to bring correction tape or fluid to make some of your mistakes disappear when you proofread. If the professor has provided a study guide, it's a good idea to have it with you and look it over one more time before class begins. And, of course, if there are any reading materials associated with the exam, bring those as well. Sometimes, your in-class essay will require you to respond to something you've read, and the professor may allow you to have access to the text or to the notes you've taken on it. Not having that material with you could make a big difference in your grade.

Try to Be as Neat as Possible. Since you're most likely writing your essay with pen and ink, do your best to write legibly. Remember that your professor is going to be reading dozens of essays, and if yours is particularly challenging to read, he or she may lose patience with you and grade the essay accordingly.

Don't Be Afraid to Ask Questions. While your professor probably won't be able to answer questions about your grammar or about whether your thesis is any good, he or she will likely be open to other questions that are aimed at clarifying the task before you. If anything about the instructions or the writing prompt is unclear to you, don't hesitate to ask for help. Others are probably wondering the same things.

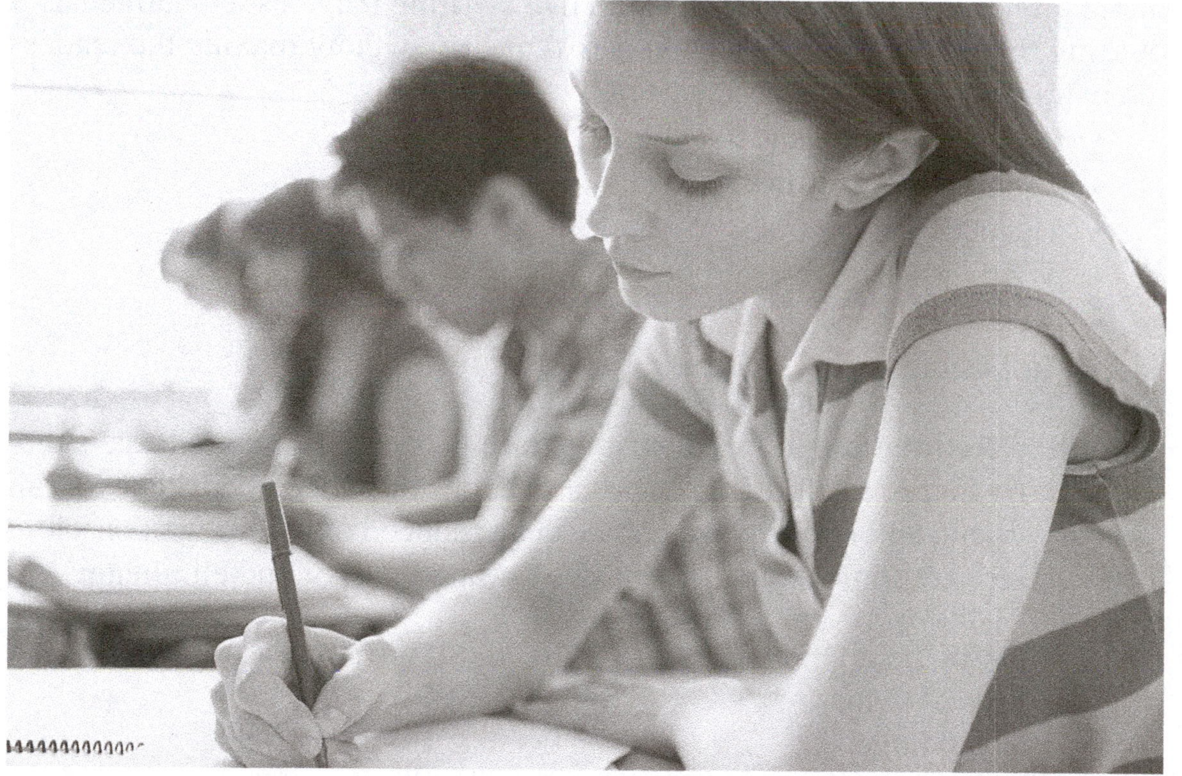

Chapter Thirteen: Writing Effective Sentences

Writing That Flows

Many students who have been discouraged by their past efforts at writing essays often claim that their writing is weak because it does not "flow." Their written language may seem choppy, or they may have been told that their sentences are awkward.

Achieving the elusive "flow" is difficult. Generally, it takes two things—practice and lots of reading. As noted in Chapter One, the more you read, the more you will develop an ear for what sounds good or bad, and with practice in revising and editing, your writing will eventually come close to approximating the language in the writing that you enjoy or admire.

There are, however, a few other things you can do to help your sentences be more effective. For the student, "effective" writing may best be defined as writing that gets the author's point across clearly without making the reader do extra work. This can be achieved by:

- Avoiding redundancy
- Eliminating wordiness
- Using specific words
- Writing with active verbs
- Avoiding clichés
- Not using sexist language

Avoiding Redundancy. A redundant phrase is one that essentially says the same thing twice. Most redundancies are the result of bad habits that we fall into as writers, and like any bad habit can be reduced only through conscious effort. Here are some redundant phrases to watch out for and eliminate:

3 pm in the afternoon
A pair of twins
Big and huge
Climb up
Each and every
Fall down
Green in color

Hurried fast
Raise up
Round in shape
Short in stature
The final conclusion
The reason why
We as humans

Your Turn

The following sentences all contain redundant phrases. Identify the problems and remove them.

1. Police reported that the armed gunman had been captured without incident.
2. I was pleased when the credit card company offered me a free gift.
3. We were worried to hear that the dog had fallen through the frozen ice, but everyone was relieved to hear that it had been rescued.
4. Fortunately, no one was hurt when the bomb in the package suddenly exploded.
5. The inspector looked at everything, examining each and every tiny speck of evidence until he had determined who the guilty criminal was.

Eliminating Wordiness. This, too, is usually the result of bad habits in writing. Sometimes, the wordy phrases may sound more sophisticated than their briefer counterparts, and the temptation may be to use the "fancy" phrase instead of the plain one. However, too much of this type of thing can lead a reader to get confused and need to re-read your sentences, causing a breakdown in communication when the reader eventually gives up. Watch out for the following phrases:

at this point in time	Now ~~At this point in time~~, we can see the need for education.
due to the fact that	Because ~~Due to the fact that~~ gas is expensive, I walk to work.
for the purpose of	to I talked to my boss ~~for the purpose of~~ get~~ting~~ a raise.

have the capability to	can Some children ~~have the capability to~~ read at an early age.
have a tendency to	Students today ~~have a~~ tend~~ency~~ to be competitive.
in spite of the fact that	even though I ate ~~in spite of the fact that~~ I was not hungry.
in the event of	During ~~In the event of~~ an earthquake, duck and cover.
in the process of	We are ~~in the process of~~ remodeling our kitchen.
on a regular basis	regularly I check my email ~~on a regular basis.~~
until such time as	We will work until ~~such time as~~ the project is completed.

Along with these phrases, you should also avoid starting sentences with "There is," "There are," or "It is." These phrases can almost always be removed from your sentences, along with one or two other words, making the whole sentence more concise. For example:

Instead of writing:

There are only two species of elephants that are still alive today.

You could write:

Only two species of elephants are still alive today.

Or, instead of:

It is possible that the disease is transmitted through the air.

Try:

The disease may be transmitted through the air.

Your Turn

The following sentences contain phrases that are unnecessarily wordy. On a separate sheet of paper, rewrite them to eliminate as many unnecessary words and phrases as possible without taking away from the meaning.

1. At this time, it is essential that we pay as close attention as is possible to the causes of the current problem.

2. Due to the fact that supporters of the new law are few in number, it seems that the only possible course of action is to assemble a committee whose purpose will be to study alternative solutions to the current problem.

3. Before making a decision in regard to the creation of new positions within the company, it came to the owner's attention that a significant negative flow of finances had raised serious doubts as to the company's future ability to continue functioning.

4. More often than not, a child will be required to master certain skills and to demonstrate said mastery before being allowed to advance to the next stage.

5. Prior to experiencing full functionality of one's automotive transport unit, it is absolutely necessary that one apply mild pressure to the security device that has been inserted into the ignition slot; that is, of course, after the aforementioned driver has taken proper care to secure the vehicle restraint system and to make all necessary adjustments to the unit's reflective apparatuses.

Using Specific Words. Consider the following sentence: "Sometimes people do things that are very bad." Grammatically, there is nothing wrong with it, but stylistically it is weak. The problem is that it is filled with vague words—*sometimes, people, things, very,* and *bad*. A reader is left wondering who these people are, what they do, and when they do it; it is also difficult to say what is meant by the word *bad* and how that is different from *very bad*. To some readers, *very bad* could mean horrible crimes, and to others it could mean forgetting to wash their hands before preparing food.

This is not effective communication, as the reader is left wondering just what the writer means.

If you find yourself using vague or general terms, replace them with specific, detailed words instead.

- Words like *good, bad*, and *nice* are open to interpretation. Say what you mean instead.
- Words like *someone, anyone, no one, sometimes, always, never, people, things, lots, a lot*, etc. are extremely unclear and completely open to the reader's interpretation. Replace with specific words. In the cases of *always* and *never*, you should be aware that there are usually exceptions to these generalizations, and once your reader thinks of a single exception to the point you're making, the generalization is no longer valid.
- Use specific nouns—*Lexus* instead of *car*; *pizza* instead of *food*; *leather jacket* instead of *clothes*; etc.
- Use specific verbs—*strut* instead of *walk*; *reek* instead of *smell*; etc.
- Avoid the use of *you* unless you literally mean the reader.
- Avoid using the adverbs *very* and *really*; they do almost nothing to enhance the meaning of what you're saying.

Your Turn

The following paragraph uses some vague words and phrases. Rewrite to make it more specific, detailed, and lively.

During the ceremony, I sat with people I had known for years. All of us were dressed the same, and we were all really uncomfortable. The weather was awful, and there were a lot of us there, so when we crowded together, it made everything worse. The whole place smelled bad, and no one seemed like they wanted to be there. I listened to all the stuff being said by the people on the stage and waited for it to be over. But when I heard my name and people clapped for me, it made everything better as I walked back to my seat.

Writing With Active Verbs. Imagine a romantic dinner with low lights, soft music, and a couple gazing into each other's eyes. When one says, "I love you" and the other responds with "You are loved by me," there is definitely a sense that something is not right here. Both phrases mean the same thing, but the first is far more direct and easier to understand. What's more, in the response, the words "by me" could be dropped, and the sentence would still be grammatically correct. The difference between the two sentences comes down to the use of active and passive verbs.

A sentence like "I lost your iPod" uses an **active verb** while "Your iPod was lost" uses a **passive verb**. The difference is that in the active sentence, there is a clear connection between the subject and the verb, the action and the person or thing doing the action. In the passive sentence, it is not clear who did what. Furthermore, the passive sentence relies on a form of "to be" for its main verb (words such as *is, are, was, were*) while the active sentence's verb has more action to it.

Be aware that passive sentences are grammatically correct. Technically, there is nothing wrong with them, and sometimes you have no choice but to use them. However, if an essay is cluttered with passive sentences, the result is that most sentences lack action (resulting in writing that seems boring), and it is also not always clear who did what (resulting in writing that may be confusing).

The easiest way to avoid passive verbs is to limit your use of "to be" verbs. If you find yourself using *is, are, was,* and *were* throughout your essay in ways other than as helping verbs (I *was driving* to school and had a flat tire) or linking verbs (I broke my arm when I *was* nine years old), then you may be using passive verbs. Try revising by flipping parts of the sentence around, eliminating the form of "to be," and changing anything else that needs changing. For example:

She was frightened by the slasher film. (passive)

The slasher film frightened her. (active)

Again, there is nothing *wrong* with the passive sentence. It is simply something to avoid when you can in order to make your writing clearer.

Your Turn

Read the following sentences and determine if they contain any passive verbs. Where you find passive constructions, revise to make them active.

1. The ring is traditionally kept by the best man.
2. It is best to move your furniture before the room is painted.
3. She was told by her boss to clear all of the accounts.
4. I walked out to my car to find that my stereo had been stolen.
5. It was on a Monday when I found out that I was going to be fired.
6. My computer was working fine until it was dropped.
7. We had a good day on the lake because the fish were biting.
8. He wouldn't say where he'd gotten the song, just that it was downloaded.
9. I walked by the lake to see if the ducks were still there.
10. She was angry that the cake had been eaten before she'd had any.

Avoiding Clichés. A cliché is an overused phrase. There may not be anything wrong with it grammatically, but it is still something you should avoid. The first time someone described hard rain by saying it was "raining cats and dogs," he or she was probably looked upon as being rather clever for coming up with such a vivid and lively description. Now, however, the phrase has become a cliché, and if you were to use it to describe hard rain, no one would give the phrase a second thought. In conversation, that may be fine, but when you write, you should strive for originality; don't rely on phrases others have come up with. They take the energy out of your paper and can label your work as unoriginal or uninspired.

Some examples of clichés include:

A whole new ballgame
As old as the hills
Black as night
Cold as ice
Cool, calm and collected
Crystal clear
Deliver the goods
Drive like a maniac
Follow in one's father's footsteps
Free as a bird
Hit the nail on the head
Hit the spot
Hungry as a horse
In the poorhouse
Last but not least
Loud as thunder
Make a federal case out of it
On thin ice
Rude awakening
Sadder but wiser
Screech to a halt

Separate the men from the boys
Short and sweet
Sick as a dog
Sparkled like diamonds
Take the cake
That gets my goat
The crack of dawn
The last straw
Tip of the iceberg
Up against a brick wall
Up to par
White as snow

When you notice a cliché in your writing, delete it and replace it with something else. The new phrase may seem a bit flat in comparison (if, for instance, you replace "he was sick as a dog" with "sicker than he had ever been"), but it is possible to come up with your own original phrase to get your point across (for example, "so sick that vultures were circling his bed"). Doing this takes more work and time than simply slipping a cliché into your sentence, but it will pay off with writing that is more effective and lively.

Your Turn

Write a paragraph in which you intentionally use five cliché phrases from the list above or that you've thought of on your own. It might be helpful to go online beforehand and do a search for lists of cliché phrases to add some variety. Once you have finished your paragraph, trade with a partner and rewrite each other's paragraphs, identifying and avoiding the clichés. Remember that your goal is to produce writing that is interesting and lively, not crowded with overused phrases. Replacing clichés with more interesting choices usually results in writing that is a bit longer than writing that is choked with clichés.

Not Using Sexist Language. There was a time when language we now consider sexist would have been appropriate in an academic setting. For example, it would have been fine to write, "If a student wants to succeed, he should study diligently." Using *he* as a pronoun for *people* in general would have been acceptable, as it was understood that the male pronoun was being used to refer to everyone. However, in the above sentence the male pronoun by definition suggests that the student is male. While this may have been an accurate assumption several decades ago when more men than women went to college, that balance has since shifted, and to use the masculine pronoun to refer to people in general is now inaccurate and reflects an old pro-male bias. Thus, in most academic writing, it will not be acceptable to use *he* or *him* to refer to people in general, just as it is no longer acceptable to use terms like *fireman, policeman, mail man*, etc. It is more acceptable to use *he or she*. If this seems awkward, switch your nouns and pronouns to plurals and use the gender-neutral *they*, *them,* or *their*. Better yet, use specific names and avoid the problem altogether.

For example, here is a sentence using sexist language:

> A doctor will always do his best to give patients the information they need.

The sentence could be revised this way:

> Doctors will always do their best to give patients the information they need.

Chapter Fourteen: Using the Best Words

In revising your writing, one part of the process involves looking carefully and closely at the words you have chosen to convey your ideas to your reader. In Chapter Thirteen, we considered writing effective sentences. Now, we will take a look at specific words. To help yourself choose and use the best, most effective words in your essays, you need to consider the words' **connotations** and **denotations**.

Connotations

A word's connotations are the feelings or sense that the word conveys, usually expressed as **positive** or **negative connotations**. This is different from the meaning of a word. In fact, two words can *mean* the same thing while having different connotations.

For example, *aquarium* and *fish tank* could be used to describe the same thing—the place where someone keeps pet fish. Thus, the **meaning** of both terms may be the same, but the connotations are different—with *aquarium* sounding more technical and proper than *fish tank*, which seems casual and non-scientific.

Consider another example: the difference between *house* and *home*. If one actually does live in a house, the two terms would have the same meaning, but the sense of both words is different. *Home* has more positive connotations than *house*; *home* seems more comforting and welcoming than *house*.

Here is one last example: would someone be more likely to say he or she lives on a *dead end street* or a *cul-de-sac*? Most people would probably prefer the second term, which, being French, may seem more cultured and classy. At the very least, it does not have the negative connotations associated with *dead* or anything else related to death.

Your writing will be stronger if you pay attention to the connotations of the words you choose, avoiding terms that do not fit the tone or subject you are writing about. In an essay describing the beginning of a relationship, this sentence would seem out of place:

> After a nice dinner and a walk along the pier, we terminated our date just before midnight.

Here, *terminate* would not be the best word to use as it has negative connotations, usually associated with death or with the sudden, forceful end of something like a job.

The problem with choosing words with inappropriate connotations usually occurs when the writer uses words that he or she is not entirely familiar with. Resist the urge to use a thesaurus, as the synonyms it points you toward may have the wrong connotations. Similarly, you will be better off if you choose words with which you are familiar.

Denotations

While a word's connotation refers to the sense it conveys, a word's **denotation** refers simply to its definition. While using a word with the wrong connotation can cause your writing to appear awkward, using the wrong denotation can cause the writing to become unclear, inaccurate and confusing. No one ever uses the wrong word intentionally—such mistakes more typically arise from misunderstandings that go uncorrected. Here, then, are some commonly confused words and explanations of the differences between them.

Accept: to agree or welcome. Example: She accepted the invitation.
Except: a word indicating something is excluded. Example: We saw every episode except the last one.

Affect: a verb meaning that something has an impact. Example: The fever affected my sleep, giving me horrible dreams.
Effect: a noun referring to the impact something has. Example: I felt the effects of a sleepless night all the next day.
Note: You can remember the difference by thinking about **special** ***effects*** in the movies—explosions, car crashes, etc., are **things** you see and these are nouns.

A lot: a two-word phrase meaning a large amount. Example: I have a lot of reading to do this weekend.
Alot: not Standard English. Avoid using this.

Alright: not Standard English. Avoid using this.
All right: a two-word phrase meaning that everything is acceptable or correct.

Apart: something is separate from something else. Example: The veterinarian tries to keep the dogs and cats apart.
A part: a component. Example: He finally became a part of the band.

At least: a two-word phrase, meaning the minimum or the slightest degree of something. Example: The doctor said I should stay home for at least two days.
Atleast: not Standard English. Avoid using this.

Definitely: an adverb indicating that something is done with certainty. Example: I am definitely going to quit my job.
Defiantly: an adverb indicating that something is done in defiance. Example: She defiantly stood up to her abusive boss.

Each other: a two-word phrase indicating a mutual exchange. Example: Everyone at the ceremony gave each other hugs.
Eachother: not Standard English. Avoid using this.

Etc.: abbreviation for the Latin *et cetera*, meaning *and also*. Example: I enjoy outdoor activities like hiking, skiing, snowboarding, etc.
Ect.: not Standard English. Avoid using this

Granted: something is treated as a given or a constant. Example: we take it for granted that the sun will rise in the morning.
Granite: a type of rock. **Don't write**: My boss takes me for granite.

Hopefully: an adverb describing the hopeful way something is done. Example: The congregation prayed hopefully for the health of their leader.
Hopeful: an adjective describing a feeling of hope. Example: I am hopeful that I will pass this class.

It's: abbreviation for *it is* or *it has*. Example: Now it's time to say goodbye.
Its: possessive form of *it*. Example: The dog chased its tail.

Know: to have knowledge or understanding. Example: I know what I'm supposed to do.
No: a word indicating the negative. Example: The printer had no more ink.
Now: a word indicating the present. Example: I need to go home right now.

Loose: an adjective describing something that is not tight or constricting. Example: I always wear loose clothing when I go to the gym.
Lose: a verb indicating that something has been lost. Example: If we lose this game, I'm quitting the team.

Nowadays: a casual way of saying *these days*. Example: Nowadays, more families rely on both parents working.
Now and days: not Standard English. Avoid using this.
Now in days: not Standard English. Avoid using this.

Possess: a verb indicating ownership. Example: After years of hard work, I was finally able to possess a car.
Posses: the plural of posse.

Quiet: something that is almost silent, not noisy. Example: Because they are quiet, lizards make good pets for people in apartments.
Quite: a word indicating a strong degree of something. Example: I was quite surprised when I won the lottery.
Quit: to stop doing something. Example: I quit watching television when my grades fell.

Supposed to: a phrase indicating that something is expected. Example: We were supposed to be here at noon.
Suppose to: not Standard English. Avoid using this.

Than: a word used for comparison. Example: The Magna Charta is older than the Constitution.
Then: a word indicating time or sequence of events. Example: She fell asleep, and then she dreamed.

There: a word indicating location or starting a sentence with an interjection. Example: My car is over there. Or: There are many ways we could solve this problem.
Their: a word indicating plural possession. Example: The politicians gave their promise to the voters.
They're: a contraction of *they are*. Example: They're in business together.

Used to: a phrase indicating past actions or something that has become commonplace. Example: We used to shop there, but now the prices are too high. Or: After a few weeks, my cat got used to taking baths.
Use to: not Standard English. Avoid using this.

Who: used to replace the subject in a clause or phrase. Example: The doctor who saw me last week was out today, so I saw another one.
Whom: used to replace the object in a clause or phrase. Example: I emailed the classmate with whom I had been studying. Or: The guy whom I've been dating is moving to Alaska.

Woman: one adult female. Example: My mother is a strong woman.
Women: more than one adult female. Example: There are several women in my math class.

Your: a pronoun expressing possession in the second person. Example: Remember not to leave your books at home.
You're: a contraction of *you are*. Example: It looks like you're almost finished with that book.

Your Turn

Looking over the list of commonly confused words in the previous pages, choose five that you have had some difficulty with in the past. Using those words, write four sentences that use the words correctly and one sentence in which you intentionally use the word incorrectly. Now trade papers with a partner and try to identify the incorrect sentence and repair it. When you are finished, check each other's paper to see if the errors were caught.

Chapter Fifteen: Avoiding Common Grammar Problems

Most problems with grammar occur because the writer never learned the rules formally and has been used to writing what sounds right without being able to explain whether it is actually right or wrong. Bad habits in grammar are reinforced when students do not read much or when they read only material that is written in non-Standard English, such as emails, text messages, or some material on the Internet. In most cases, native speakers of English have only a few grammatical trouble spots and do not really need to be able to explain why they are using correct grammar. However, when grammatical errors form a pattern or a habit, overcoming these problems requires some re-thinking and re-training, and an understanding of some of the rules of grammar.

Here are a few of the most common trouble spots for students:

- Sentence Boundaries
- Pronouns
- Subject-Verb Agreement
- Verb Tense Shifts
- Modifiers
- Parallel Structure
- Commas
- Quotation Marks
- Apostrophes

In the following pages, you'll find explanations of what these problems are and how to avoid them in your writing. As far as *why* these things are problems, the basic answer is that they can cause a break in communication. If you know what you want to say, but your grammar causes your reader to have problems understanding what you mean, then you're not communicating effectively. Furthermore, grammar errors can be extremely distracting to readers who do know the rules, and since it's important for you to keep your audience in mind when you write, working on good grammar habits is key to communicating with that audience effectively.

Sentence Boundaries

Sentence boundary errors are among the most common but also among the most serious errors that find their way into students' papers. Consider this group of words:

> The foot of a parrot is different from that of all other birds

This looks like a sentence; it has a subject and a verb. But it is missing a key component: a period at the end. If there were a period after *birds*, then the writer would be sending a signal that everything before the period was a sentence. Without the boundary of the period, the reader does not have a clear understanding of where the sentence stops or starts. There are specific rules about where the boundaries lie and how to connect multiple ideas in a single sentence. There are three types of sentence boundary errors:

- Sentence Fragments
- Comma Splices
- Fused Sentences

Sentence Fragments
There are two main causes of sentence fragments:

1) A sentence is missing a subject or a verb. Usually this is because the writer has accidentally left out the subject or verb.

   This usually occurs when we have lists of things or develop examples as follow-up ideas to a previous sentence. Here is an example:

   > Sometimes we don't always know which classes are more important to enroll in because we have so many choices. Such as English, Math, Philosophy, History and Chemistry, to name a few.

   Here the second sentence is a fragment because it is just a string of nouns with no verb. It should be connected to the first sentence like this:

   > Sometimes we don't always know which classes are more important to enroll in because we have so many choices, such

as English, Math, Philosophy, History and Chemistry, to name a few.

A similar problem can occur when we use the –ing form of a verb to start a sentence. For example:

Living in Los Angeles, a city of several million people with a diversity of cultures.

In this sentence, “Living in Los Angeles” is a noun phrase, essentially a long subject that has no verb. It could be corrected by adding a verb phrase as follows:

Living in Los Angeles, a city of several million people with a
S
diversity of cultures, allows one to experience interesting
V
things.

2) The other main type of fragment is a sentence that is actually what’s called a dependent clause. That is, there is something in the sentence that causes it to depend on some other piece of information that is not in the sentence.

This is more difficult to catch and requires more explanation:

The first thing to figure out is what a **clause** is:

- A clause is any group of words that has a subject and a verb. For example:

  Fred works.
  S V

There are two types of clauses—independent clauses and dependent clauses.

Independent clause: a group of words with a subject and verb that does not need to be attached to anything else in order for it to make sense. The clause above—*Fred works*—is an example of an independent clause.

Dependent clause: a group of words with a subject and a verb that does not make sense all by itself. Usually this is because a specific type of word has been attached to an independent clause. For example:

Because Fred works. Or When Fred works.
S V S V

In these cases, the addition of *because* or *when* turns an independent clause into a dependent clause.

Just as a dependent person (such as an infant) must be attached to an independent person (such as a parent) in order to survive, so must the dependent clause be attached to an independent clause. Otherwise, the dependent clause all by itself is a fragment.

Dependent clause: When Fred works. (fragment)
S V

Independent clause: He makes money.
S V

Combined: When Fred works, he makes money.
S V S V
(dependent) + (independent) = complete sentence

In these examples, *when* and *because* are part of a group words called **subordinating conjunctions**.

Any time you use a subordinating conjunction, you are creating a dependent clause that *must* be attached to an independent clause in order for it to be part of a complete sentence. If you use a subordinating conjunction to create a dependent clause, but you do not attach it to an independent clause, then it is a fragment.

Here is a list of subordinating conjunctions:

After	If	When
Although	Since	Whenever
Because	Though	Where
Before	Unless	Whereas
Even though	Until	While

In addition to subordinating conjunctions, there is another way to make a dependent clause and which can also cause a fragment. This involves words that are called **relative pronouns**. These are:

Who/Whom Which That Whoever/Whomever Whose

Let's say you have two short sentences that you would like to combine:

> Fred works at McDonald's.
> He eats lots of French fries.

You could combine them with the relative clause *who*:

> Fred, who works at McDonald's, eats a lot of French fries.

Now, the relative clause *who* replaces the subject *he* in one of the original sentences, so *who* is acting as the subject in one of the clauses. Think of it this way:

> Fred, who works at McDonald's, eats a lot of French fries.
> **S S V V**

The problem with sentence fragments and this type of sentence usually occurs when the relative clause is longer and the writer forgets to add a verb phrase to complete the original independent clause.

For example, let's say you wanted to combine these two sentences:

Fred lives in Los Angeles, a city of several million with a diversity of
S V
cultures.

Fred enjoys meeting lots of different people.
S V

Combining the sentences this way would result in a fragment:

> Fred, who lives in Los Angeles, a city of several million with a diversity of cultures. He enjoys meeting lots of different people.

The first sentence would be a fragment because the subject in the first clause no longer is connected to a verb. Even though there is a verb in the first sentence—*lives*—it is actually connected to the relative pronoun *who* and not the subject *Fred.*

Fred, who lives in Los Angeles, a city of several million with a diversity of cultures.

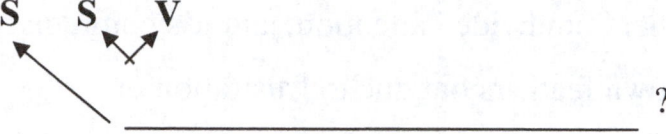

The correct way to combine these sentences would be:

> Fred, who lives in Los Angeles, a city of several million people with a diversity of cultures, enjoys meeting lots of different people.

Now the subject *Fred* has a verb—*enjoys*—and the sentence is no longer a fragment.

Your Turn

The following paragraph contains some sentence fragments. Read the paragraph, identify the fragments, and revise to eliminate the errors. Remember that fragments can often be corrected by connecting the fragment to the sentence that comes before or after it.

The blue-headed pionus parrot would make an ideal pet bird for someone living in an apartment. Or perhaps would make a great starter bird for someone not used to parrots. Unlike macaws and amazons, which have a tendency to be noisy and to squawk loudly when they are bored, lonely, or just feeling particularly happy. The blue-headed pionus tends to be much quieter. While it is true that these birds may squawk with joy when first getting up in the morning. Their noise is generally not as bad as with other birds. Along with not being too noisy, these birds are also smaller than their cousins and so don't take up as much room. Additionally, the pi (as their owners affectionately refer to them) is a rather low-maintenance bird. Content to sit and look out the window for hours at a time and happy just to have its human companions in the same room with it. Other birds get insecure without a lot of attention. Cocaktoos, for instance. These birds are notorious for wanting their owners' undivided attention, and it's common for some cockatoos to pluck their own feathers out due to frustration or loneliness. These social problems are rarely found in the blue-headed pi.

Comma Splices and Fused Sentences

Once you understand what independent and dependent clauses are, you have also gained the key to avoiding comma splices and fused sentences. Here are the definitions previously explained:

> **Independent clause:** a group of words with a subject and verb that does not need to be attached to anything else in order for it to make sense.
>
> **Dependent clause:** a group of words with a subject and a verb that does not make sense all by itself. Usually this is because a specific type of word has been attached to an independent clause.

Comma splices and fused sentences occur when we incorrectly combine independent clauses. If they are combined with a comma, the result is a comma splice. For example:

My car stalled, I called my sister for a ride.
S V S V

If two independent clauses are combined with no connecting punctuation at all, it is a fused sentence. Some instructors call this a run-on sentence.

My car stalled I called my sister for a ride.
S V S V

To correct comma splices and fused sentences, you need to make sure you combine them correctly. There are a few ways to do this.

1. You can turn one of the independent clauses into a dependent clause by using a subordinating conjunction:

When my car stalled, I called my sister for a ride.
Dependent Independent

2. You can combine the independent clauses with a semi-colon:

My car stalled; I called my sister for a ride.

3. You can use a coordinating conjunction and a comma to connect the independent clauses. Here is a list of coordinating conjunctions:

for
and
nor
but
or
yet
so

If you read down the first letters of each of these words, they spell out *fanboys*. This may help you remember the coordinating conjunctions. To avoid comma splices and fused sentences using coordinating conjunctions, combine the two independent clauses with a comma and whichever one of the *fanboys* that makes sense. For example:

My car stalled, and I called my sister for a ride.

Or

My car stalled, so I called my sister for a ride.

4. The fourth way to avoid comma splices and fused sentences is to make each independent clause into its own sentence:

My car stalled. I called my sister for a ride.

Be aware, however, that separating all of your sentences this way could make your writing seem choppy, so try to use different methods of combining clauses for a smoother effect.

Your Turn

The following paragraph contains some comma splices and fused sentences. Read the paragraph, identify the errors, and revise to eliminate them.

In 1962, a new sound could be heard on the AM radios of the cars that cruised up and down California's Pacific Coast Highway. While most songs were by the popular singers of the day, there would occasionally be the energetic pounding of guitar-based instrumentals, surf music had been born. Many point to Dick Dale as the founding father of the new music. A self-taught guitarist, Dale played left-handed he had never learned that left-handed guitarists were supposed to reverse the order of the strings from thinnest to fattest. As a result, Dale basically played the guitar upside down, but his strange method led to a unique style. Along with being a musician, he was also a surfer, he tried to capture the feeling of surfing in his music. With the reverb turned up all the way on his amplifier, Dale entertained his fans with songs like "Let's Go Trippin'" and "Miserlou." Soon, other bands followed, some adding lyrics to their surf-inspired songs, however none of them could copy Dale's style. He played so fast that he would melt his guitar picks his shows were so loud that he blew out thirty amplifiers before the Fender guitar company designed an amplifier that could withstand him. It was no wonder that he was called "King of the Surf Guitar."

Pronouns

Pronouns are words that we use to take the place of nouns. Without pronouns, we would have to repeat words continuously when we write. This would get awkward and annoying rather quickly. For example:

When Justine phoned Justine's husband, Jake, Justine asked Jake if Justine and Jake could meet Justine's parents for dinner at Justine's parents' house that night.

Instead, you would write:

When Justine phoned her husband, Jake, she asked him if they could meet for dinner at her parents' house that night.

Pronouns include:

I	They	Their
You	Them	Your
He	Him	Me
She	Her	My
It	His	Mine
We	Hers	

For pronouns to make sense, they have to be taking the place of a noun. The noun that is being replaced is called the **antecedent**. Problems with pronouns usually occur when there is a difference between the pronoun and the antecedent. When pronouns and antecedents correspond in number and gender, they are said to agree, and **pronoun agreement** becomes a problem when there is a difference between the gender or number of the pronoun and the antecedent it refers to. For example:

If a student studies hard enough, their grades will usually show it.

The antecedent (*student*) is singular, but the pronoun replacing it (*their*) is plural. This sentence has an agreement problem. To correct it, the number of the antecedent or the pronoun needs to change. The author could change the pronoun:

If a student studies hard enough, his grades will usually show it.

However, this sentence now has a new problem: it is using sexist language, implying that the unidentified student is male. Instead, the author could do one of the following:

If a student studies hard enough, his or her grades will usually show it.
(Use more than one pronoun to avoid sexist language.)

Or

If students study hard enough, their grades will usually show it. *(Make the antecedent plural.)*

Here is another example with a singular antecedent and a plural pronoun:

When a person thinks of California, they first imagine the sunny skies.

Again, this can be corrected by changing the antecedent or the pronoun:

When people think of California, they first imagine the sunny skies.

Or

When a person thinks of California, he or she usually imagines the sunny skies.

Another problem can occur when writers rely too heavily on the pronoun *you*. **Remember that *you* refers directly to the reader**. While it may be acceptable in informal conversation to use *you* to refer to people in general, the same does not hold true for academic writing. For example:

People with bad driving records face high insurance rates, and if you have an expensive car or live in an area that has a lot of theft, your rates will probably go even higher.

In this sentence, there is an unspoken (and probably unintended) message that the *reader* may have high insurance rates because of these conditions. Instead of using *you*, use a pronoun that matches the antecedent:

People with bad driving records face high insurance rates, and if they have an expensive car or live in an area that has a lot of theft, their rates will probably go even higher.

The word *everyone* also causes problems with pronoun agreement. Consider this example:

Everyone hopes their children will grow up to be happy people.

Here, *everyone* is the antecedent for the pronoun *their*. However, the problem is that the pronoun is plural while the antecedent noun is singular. We may think of *everyone* as more than person (thus, plural), but notice that the noun *everyone* takes the **singular** form of the verb *hopes* (more on this below). So while we are thinking of lots and lots of people when we write *everyone*, we actually are referring to *every single individual*. So we need to make sure the pronoun is singular as well; and while we might be tempted to use the pronoun *his* in this situation, we also need to be careful not to use sexist language. The correct way to write the sentence, then, would be:

> Everyone hopes his or her children will grow up to be happy people.

Now our pronouns are singular to match the singular antecedent. If using *his or her* or something similar seems awkward to you, or if you find yourself using that phrase over and over, then you should consider revising to avoid *everyone*. After all, the word is incredibly general, technically referring to billions of people, and your essay would probably be stronger if it focused on something more specific.

One other problem often occurs with pronouns. This has to do with **unclear pronoun reference**. In other words, the reader may have difficulty knowing what the **antecedent** is for a particular pronoun. Remember that the antecedent is the word that the pronoun is replacing. In this sentence, the relationship between the pronoun and antecedent is clear:

> My boss called this morning, and he said I could come in an hour later than normal.

Here, *boss* is the noun, or antecedent, for the pronoun *he*, so when we read this sentence, we know whom the pronoun refers to. Compare with this sentence:

> My roommate told me that my boss called, and he said I could come in an hour later than normal.

While the message is basically the same in this sentence, readers don't know if the writer refers to the boss or the roommate when using the pronoun *he*. This is not a huge problem, but enough of these errors can cause the writing to be imprecise and can lead readers to become confused. Remember that your goal is to communicate clearly with your reader, and unclear references like the one above can cause a breakdown in that communication.

Here is another example where the meaning becomes even more vague:

> I wanted to plant the red rose bush next to the white one, but it died.

In this example, we know that one of the rose bushes died, but we don't know which one since the antecedent for the pronoun *it* is unclear. The problem could be solved in different ways, but the main thing to keep in mind is that the reader needs to know which noun the pronoun refers to. Here is one way to make the sentence clearer:

> The red rose bush died before I could plant it next to the white one.

Another problem with pronouns and antecedents occurs when there simply is no antecedent. Most often, this happens when the writer assumes the reader will understand what the pronoun refers to. For example:

> Bicyclists must always be on the lookout for cars, since they aren't always aware of bicycles sharing the road with them.

In this sentence, the pronouns *they* and *them* seem to refer to the cars' drivers, but those drivers are not in the sentence, so the pronouns technically have no antecedent and are thus incorrect. Too many problems like this will cause readers to get confused.

Your Turn

The following paragraph has a variety of pronoun errors. Identify the problems and revise to correct them.

When a person goes to eBay on the internet, they find themselves in the middle of a huge, nationwide yard sale where sellers mix treasure with junk and offer it to the highest bidder. You can find everything from antiques to everyday household items, and they can be had for pennies or for fortunes depending on who else is bidding on them along with you. Everyone has old things around the house that they could get rid of, and eBay is a great way to sell it for a few dollars rather than just throw it away. If a buyer needs something, and the stores charge more than you want to pay, they should always check the auction site to see if it is available. The chances are good that there will be a seller somewhere with the same item for sale, and they will likely be offering it for less than they had it in the stores.

Subject-Verb Agreement

In English, writers do not have to worry about conjugating their verbs as much as writers must in other languages like French or Spanish. However, there is one case where we do need to pay attention to verb endings. This occurs when we use a third-person singular noun with a present-tense verb.

I work.	(first person)
You work.	(second person singular)
We work.	(second person plural)
He/She/It **works**.	(third person singular)
They work	(third person plural)

Native speakers of English generally don't have a problem with this. However, when there is something separating the subject from the verb, it can be easy to get confused, and the resulting mismatch of subject and verb can lead to a problem with agreement. For example:

When an employer, perhaps out of arrogance or poor management
S
skills, ask unreasonable things of employees, the result can be
V
unpleasant.

Here, you have a singular subject (*employer*) and a verb form (*ask*) that does not match. Instead, the sentence should read:

When an employer, perhaps out of arrogance or poor management skills, **asks** unreasonable things of employees, the result can be unpleasant.

Careful proofreading can help you avoid this type of error. If you find think your subjects and their matching verbs are a bit far from each other, try to match them up and then make sure that any third-person singular subjects have matching verbs.

This is also a good example of an area of writing where the grammar checker on your computer may be of no help to you, since the software may see a plural noun (like *skills* in the example above) next to the verb and think they go together—when in fact that verb should have been matched with the singular noun (*employer*) that came earlier.

Another potential trouble spot with subject-verb agreement comes along when we use **collective nouns**. These are nouns where more than one person or thing is referred to with a single word.

There are several collective nouns in English, but the ones you're most likely to encounter in your essays would be:

Audience	Group
Class	Jury
Faculty	Staff
Family	Team

Making these nouns agree with their verbs gets tricky only when you're using them in the present tense. In that case, you need to ask yourself if the collective is acting as a single unit, or if each member of the collective is acting individually. For instance, if everyone in a family has dinner at the same time, you could say the family is acting as a unit, but if each person eats separately, then the members are acting individually.

The family eats together every night at six-thirty. (singular noun with singular verb)

The family eat dinner one at a time, whenever each person has a moment to throw some food together. (Plural noun with plural verb. This does sound awkward, but it is correct.)

Your Turn

Read the following paragraph and look for errors in subject-verb agreement.

These days, multi-tasking has become the normal way of doing things. A person who has many friends and close co-workers want to get in touch with them regularly and so will connect with them on Facebook or Twitter or through email while doing other tasks. A student with a term paper due sits at the computer and downloads songs in one application and research his or her topic in another. But just how useful is all this supposed productivity? We hear about accidents caused by drivers who are texting or on the phone, and the student who does other things while writing sometimes find that his or her paper is just a collection of paragraphs rather than a clearly written essay. If a family use their laptops during dinner to catch up with their friends or jobs or schoolwork, are they really still acting like a family?

Verb Tense Shifts

Using the correct verb tense is something that most native speakers of English don't have a problem with. You may have been taught the subtle differences between the past tense (*I had a problem*), the past perfect tense (*I have had a problem*), and the past perfect progressive tense (*I had been having a problem*), but unless you are an English Major, you're probably not going to need to be able to identify the tenses or explain the differences between them. More importantly, as a native speaker you likely have a natural instinct for which verb tense to use in your writing without knowing the formal name of each one.

The problem with verb tenses in your writing doesn't really have anything to do with knowing what each tense is called. Rather, it's usually a problem of shifting from one tense to another without meaning to. This typically happens when we are using detailed narrative examples in our writing and we slip back and forth between past tense and present tense verbs. Some students try to write personal narrative in the present tense because they think it sounds more exciting. In this example, the present tense verbs are in bold:

> I **am** still two miles from the finish line, and I **feel** my legs beginning to cramp. My family **is** waiting for me at the end of the course, and I **can't** let them down, but at the same time I **know** there **is** no way my tortured legs will keep me moving. Failure **is** not an option, but I **feel** as though continuing will only **cause** my exhausted body to break down. I **have** no choice. Gritting my teeth, I **keep** my legs moving, focusing only on the next step and then the one after it. The pain **doesn't** get any better, but it **doesn't** get any worse, and in what **seems** like only a few minutes, I **am** through with one more mile, and I **know** I can make it.

In this example, the decision to use present tense verbs pays off, as the action seems like it's happening right now as we read. However, a whole essay in this verb tense might get tedious for the reader. More importantly, it is extremely difficult to keep this up as a writer. Our natural tendency is to tell stories in the past tense. If something happened in the past and is over now, we categorize it as a completed action, and most writers will slip into the past tense while trying to write with present tense verbs. This is a serious problem since the shifts from present tense to past tense are confusing for the reader.

As a rule, whatever verb tense you start with is the one you should use throughout. It's not wrong to use present tense verbs as in the example above; the key is to be consistent.

Here's how the above paragraph might read in a student's essay. Incorrect verb choices are written in *italics*.

> I **am** still two miles from the finish line, and I **feel** my legs beginning to cramp. My family ***was*** waiting for me at the end of the course, and I ***couldn't*** let them down, but at the same time I ***knew*** there ***was*** no way my tortured legs will keep me moving. Failure **is** not an option, but I **feel** as though continuing will only **cause** my exhausted body to

> break down. I **have** no choice. Gritting my teeth, I **keep** my legs moving, focusing only on the next step and then the one after it. The pain ***didn't*** get any better, but it ***didn't*** get any worse, and in what ***seemed*** like only a few minutes, I **am** through with one more mile, and I **know** I can make it.

As you can see, the effect is rather confusing, but the problem can almost always be taken care of by avoiding the use of present tense verbs in narration or examples. If you want your writing to sound exciting, that effect is best achieved through your choice of interesting and specific verbs and adjectives.

Modifiers

A modifier is a word or phrase that changes or adds to the meaning of something. Modifiers are usually **adjectives** or **adverbs** or phrases that function as adjectives or adverbs. As with verb tenses, most native speakers of English use modifiers correctly without being able to identify what part of speech they are using. However, along with that intuitive understanding can also come some bad habits and possibly some sloppy constructions that can lead to writing that is unclear or incorrect.

To understand the problems associated with modifiers and how to correct or avoid them, it is necessary first to refresh your memory on the basic parts of speech.

Noun	a person, place, thing or concept	My **dog** ate my **homework**.
Verb	an action word OR	My dog **ate** my homework.
	a word that links parts of a sentence	My dog **was** hungry.
Adjective	a word describing a noun	My homework was **brilliant**, but my **hungry** dog ate it.
Adverb	a word describing an adjective, verb or another adverb	My homework was **completely** brilliant, but my **incredibly** hungry dog **foolishly** ate it.

Notice how the adverbs and adjectives add layers of meaning and understanding to the words they modify, making the language more vivid and specific. Notice, too, that the modifiers are placed as closely as possible to the words they modify. If the modifier is separated from the word it modifies, the result can be confusing. For example,

> Foolishly, my homework was completely brilliant, but my incredibly hungry dog ate it.

Here, it's difficult to know just what the word *foolishly* is doing in the sentence. Is it supposed to refer to the dog, the homework, or the writer who allowed the hungry dog access to the homework? When you write a sentence in which it's unclear what the connection is between the modifier and the thing being modified, the result is rather muddy, and the reader is left trying to figure out what the writer means. Making your reader do extra work like this is a quick way to make the reader lose interest. At the very least, you've given the reader an opportunity to determine for him or herself just what you mean, which is not the most effective way to communicate. Instead, you need to be more in command, ensuring that your readers get the point you intended them to get. Making sure you're controlling your modifiers is one way to achieve this.

Here are some tricky modifiers that can cause your writing to be unclear.

Modifiers That Limit. This group of modifiers includes words like *only, almost, hardly,* and *just* as well as others that put limitations on the things being modified. If you put these words in the wrong place in your sentence, you can unintentionally change the meaning. Notice how putting the modifier *only* in different places can affect the meaning of a sentence:

Only Tim can solve this problem.	(meaning: there is no one other than Tim who can solve the problem)
Tim can only solve this problem.	(meaning: Tim can't do anything except solve the problem)
Tim can solve only this problem.	(meaning: Tim can't solve any other problems)

Each of these sentences is grammatically correct, but if they don't convey the meaning that the writer intends, then there's a problem. Here are a few more examples:

> The cat **almost** attacked every bird in the park. (*sounds like the cat showed some restraint and didn't actually attack any birds*)
>
> The cat attacked **almost** every bird in the park. (*now the cat seems to have indulged itself and caused some problems for the birds*)
>
> I was killed **nearly** a year ago in a car accident. (*sounds like the writer has been dead for almost a year*)
>
> I was **nearly** killed a year ago in a car accident. (*now it is clear that the writer almost died and that the accident was a year ago*)

Commonly Confused Adverbs and Adjectives. We can also run into problems when we use the adverb form of a word as though it were an adjective. In these cases, most readers would understand what is meant, but technically it is still an error and should be avoided. The most commonly confused adverb/adjective pairs are:

Hopeful/Hopefully
Real/Really
Good/Well

Let's start with the first two pairs. *Hopeful* and *Real* are adjectives and *Hopefully* and *Really* are adverbs. Here's how they typically get misused.

> I was real hungry. I was real tired. It had been a real long day. Hopefully, tomorrow would be better.

Even though *real* is an adjective, it is being used in the first three sentences to modify other adjectives (*hungry, tired,* and *long*) which is the job of an adverb. Instead, *real* should be modifying a noun (remember that Pinocchio wants to be a *real boy*). In the last sentence, *hopefully* is an adverb, but it is not being used to modify a verb, adjective or another adverb. Instead, it seems to modify *tomorrow*, which is a noun and which doesn't really make sense, since *tomorrow* isn't capable of hoping for anything. The unspoken meaning of the last sentence is that the <u>writer</u> hopes tomorrow will be better, and since *writer* is a noun, it should be modified with an adjective. Here's how the sentences should read:

> I was really hungry. I was really tired. It had been a really long day. I was hopeful that tomorrow would be better.

Most speakers of English have gotten into the bad habit of using *hopefully* as an adjective instead of an adverb. Remember that if you start a sentence with *hopefully*, it is almost certainly being used incorrectly.

And, speaking of *really*, it's probably a good idea if you avoid using it as much as possible. It's overused in English and, like *very* doesn't add much to your sentences.

Consider the difference between:

The car was old.

And:

The car was really old.

Based on either of these sentences, do we really know how old the car was? Instead of using rather meaningless adverbs like *very* or *really* to modify an adjective, consider using some more vivid and specific descriptions to paint a picture for the reader:

> The dilapidated car seemed to be made more of rust than metal and looked as though it would never move again, let alone start.

We still may not know exactly how old the car is, but we do have a much better sense of how it holds its age. This gives readers a clearer picture than if we simply learned that the car was 40, or 60, or 80 years old.

Finally, we need to look at the difference between *good* and *well*. In their simplest forms, *good* is an adjective and *well* is an adverb. You can imagine having a *good time* or a *good dog*, reading a *good book* or eating *good food*. Here, *time, dog, book,* and *food* are all nouns that the adjective *good* modifies correctly. Similarly, you can *eat well, live well, sleep well*, etc. where *eat, live,* and *sleep* are verbs that can be correctly modified with the adverb *well*.

However, in some cases, *well* can act as an adjective. This happens when referring to issues of health or how suitable or proper something is. For example:

After the medicine began working, I was finally well again.

To muddy things even further, when referring to the senses, *good* is used as an adverb rather than an adjective. For example:

The pizza smelled good.

To write *The pizza smelled well* would suggest that the pizza had a nose and that the nose functioned properly—not a pleasant prospect. Consider these other examples (all correct):

The song sounds good.
The cake tastes good.
The beach looks good.
The velvet feels good.

Your Turn

In the following pairs of sentences, decide which one best expresses the intended meaning:

We only ate the fish.
We ate only the fish.
[Intended meaning: we didn't eat anything but the fish.]

We ate the only fish.
We ate the fish only.
[Intended meaning: there was a single fish, and we ate it.]

Sadly, he played the guitar.
He played the guitar sadly.
[Intended meaning: he made sad sounding music come out of the guitar.]

They had a real good time at the beach.
They had a really good time at the beach.
[Intended meaning: they enjoyed their time at the beach.]

Hopefully, I will pass the test.
I am hopeful that I will pass the test.
[Intended meaning: the student feels there is a good chance he/she passed the test.]

The wind blew down almost every tree.
The wind almost blew down every tree.
[Intended meaning: very few trees were spared by the wind.]

I feel well about buying those new shoes.
I feel good about buying those new shoes.
[Intended meaning: the speaker is glad to have bought new shoes.]

I feel well enough to go shopping.
I feel good enough to go shopping.
[Intended meaning; the speaker feels healthy enough to go shopping.]

When was the last time you cleaned the kitchen? It doesn't smell good.
When was the last time you cleaned the kitchen? It doesn't smell well.
[Intended meaning: there is an unpleasant smell in the kitchen.]

Along with single adjectives and adverbs, we also use **adjective phrases** and **adverb phrases** to modify parts of our sentences.

A sentence with an adjective: He drove a **muddy** truck.
A sentence with an adjective phrase: He drove a truck **covered in mud**.
A sentence with an adverb: He drove **recklessly**.
A sentence with an adverb phrase: He drove **in a reckless manner**.

When using these phrases or single adverbs and adjectives, we can run into some interesting problems:

- **Misplaced modifiers**
- **Squinting modifiers**
- **Dangling modifiers**

Let's look briefly at each one.

Misplaced Modifiers. As with the examples above, a modifier that is not in the right place can lead to confusion. We've already looked at examples where single modifiers can cause problems. Now consider these examples with modifying phrases:

Incorrect	Correct
Getting out of the shower, I answered the phone **dressed in a towel**.	Getting out of the shower and **dressed in a towel**, I answered the phone.
Not paying attention, he let the shopping cart roll over her foot **full of groceries**.	Not paying attention, he let the shopping cart **full of groceries** roll over her foot.
Not strong enough to withstand the storm, she got drenched when her umbrella broke.	**Not strong enough to withstand the storm**, her umbrella broke, and she got drenched.

Again, the key to placing your modifiers correctly is to put them as close as possible to the word or phrase being modified.

Squinting Modifiers. A modifier is said to squint when it could refer to more than one word or phrase, usually on either side of it. For example:

Squinting: Speaking German **clearly** is difficult. (*Is it difficult to speak German clearly, or is it clearly difficult to speak German?*)

Not Squinting: **Clearly**, speaking German is difficult.
Or: It is difficult to speak German **clearly**.

Squinting: The children who got on the bus **sadly** waved goodbye. (*Did the children get on the bus sadly, or did they wave sadly?*)

Not Squinting: The children **sadly** got on the bus and waved goodbye.
Or: The children got on the bus and **sadly** waved goodbye.

Squinting: The doctor asked me to explain my symptoms **when we walked into the office**. (*Did the doctor ask the patient to wait to explain until they had walked in, or did the doctor ask for the explanation upon entering?*)

> **Not Squinting**: **When we walked into the office**, the doctor asked me to explain my symptoms.
> **Or**: The doctor asked me not to explain my symptoms **until we walked into the office**.

If you notice that a modifier or modifying phrase may be squinting, decide what you intend it to mean, and revise the sentence accordingly.

Dangling Modifiers. As with pronouns that are missing their antecedent, when a sentence includes a modifier without mentioning the thing being modified, it is incorrect and can lead to confusion. This is an easy mistake to make, especially when writing paragraphs in which our thoughts flow into each other from one sentence to the next. Consider this example:

> Sonia was having a wonderful time at the music festival. During a break between acts, she left her friends for a few minutes. **While standing in line for the restroom**, her favorite band came onstage.

Placed within the context of the other sentences, readers understand that Sonia is the one standing in line. However, from a grammatical standpoint, we have a modifying phrase (*while standing in line for the restroom*) in a sentence that does not include the thing being modified (*Sonia*). The result is that it sounds like the band was standing in line for the restroom and appearing onstage at the same time. Again, this is an easy mistake to make, and it takes a careful proofreader to catch an error like this. If you've run into this problem, the key is to make sure that the thing being modified is actually in the sentence containing the modifier.

Here are a few more examples:

> Looking out across the desert, the sand dunes cast giant shadows. (*Sounds like the dunes were looking across the desert.*)
> Walking down the street, a tree fell in my path. (*Sounds like the tree was walking.*)
> Worn out by exercise, the couch looked very inviting. (*Sounds like the couch was exercising.*)
> Eaten by a predator, Professor Jones studied the remains. (*Sounds like the professor was eaten.*)

Your Turn

Identify the misplaced, squinting and dangling modifiers in the following paragraph and revise to correct the problems. In cases where modifiers squint, decide on the best meaning for the sentence and revise accordingly.

It was the worst camping trip I ever went on. First, we had to hike eight miles into the forest with backpacks full of gear. Weighing at least forty pounds each, we were all responsible for our own things. The trail was difficult—uphill most of the way and winding through a canyon carved by a river. Then it started to rain. Falling in huge drops, we got our raingear to protect ourselves from the storm from our backpacks. Exhausted, we finally reached the campsite and began to unpack. That was when I found I'd left half of my tent poles back in the car. Shaking with frustration, the trail seemed twice as long on my way back for the poles. I decided when the trip was over I would never go camping again.

Parallel Structure

You probably remember from your math classes that two lines are *parallel* when they run in exactly the same direction at the same angle and never meet. *Parallel Structure* in writing follows a similar principle: two or more items listed in a sentence must use the same grammatical form—similar to going in the same direction at the same angle. In other words, if the first items in a series are adjectives, the rest should be adjectives, too. If you are using –ing words to explain something, then all the words in the list should take the –ing form. If you are using a list of clauses, they, too, should follow the same format rather than having a mix of active and passive clauses, for instance. Here are some examples:

Words in a series.

- Her favorite foods are **shrimp, pasta, and sushi**. (Parallel)

- Her favorite foods are shrimp, pasta, and <u>eating</u> sushi. (Not parallel)

- Since his eye surgery, he has a hard time **reading, writing, and watching** television. (Parallel)
- Since his eye surgery, he has a hard time reading, writing, and <u>to watch</u> television. (Not parallel)

- We worked **slowly, efficiently, and diligently**. (Parallel)
- We worked slowly, efficiently, and <u>in a diligent way.</u> (Not parallel)

- This year, Jennifer decided to quit her job, to go back to school, and to become an astronaut. (Parallel)

    Note: when using the infinitive form (to + simple verb) in a list, it is acceptable to use the *to* in only the first item in the list.
- This year, Jennifer decided to **quit her job, go back to school, and become an astronaut**. (Parallel)
- This year, Jennifer decided to quit her job, go back to school, and <u>becoming</u> an astronaut. (Not parallel)

    Note: remember to keep your verb forms the same in lists like this.
- This year, Jennifer decided to quit her job, go back to school, and <u>became</u> an astronaut. (Not parallel)

Clauses in a series.

- Ed needed a computer that had enough memory to run complex software, that could store large files, and <u>to connect</u> constantly to the Internet. (Not parallel)
- Ed needed a computer **that had enough memory** to run complex software, **that could store** large files, and **that would connect** constantly to the Internet. (Parallel)
- In school today, we watched a film that was emotionally overpowering, that told a compelling story, and <u>a few students were upset by it</u>. (Not parallel)

- In school today, we watched a film **that was emotionally overpowering, that told a compelling story, and that upset a few students**. (Parallel)

Your Turn

The following paragraph contains several sentences with faulty parallelism. Correct the errors.

These days, when people talk about the achievements women have made in Hollywood and the film industry, they often focus on the idea that these women are daring, gutsy, and have taken their positions in a business that has excluded women or kept them from gaining power for a long time. Few people realize, however, that when the American film industry began, there were many powerful women who wrote, directed and films were produced by them as well. In the 1910s and 1920s, it was more common for women than for men to write the scenarios for silent films. Writing was a job considered acceptable, appropriate, and no one objected to hiring women to put together stories for the new industry. As a result many early films portrayed strong female characters, tackled issues important to the women of the period, and have given viewers a new perspective when watching those films today. One of the most successful screenwriters of the time was Frances Marion, who began as an actress and soon found herself on the other side of the camera. By the time she ended her career, she had won several Academy Awards, had earned a reputation for being one of the best writers in the industry, and she was close friends with some of the most powerful people in Hollywood. She also directed her own movies, often starring her good friend Mary Pickford, herself a film pioneer who went on to co-found United Artists, a production company that made films for decades.

Commas

For some reason, commas tend to give students a lot of trouble. When asked, they often say they simply don't know where the commas go, and so students put them in "wherever it feels right." Some students have fallen victim to their teachers' red pens, having their commas marked wrong, and so hesitate to put any commas into their work for fear of being graded harshly again. Many people were told in elementary school to put commas into sentences where the reader would naturally pause. The problem with all of these formulas for using commas is that they are arbitrary. We don't all pause in the same places, and it doesn't always "feel right" to put a comma in one spot or another; simply avoiding commas is also a sure way to run into difficulties.

Instead, you need to learn some simple rules for comma usage. There's nothing mystical about it.

You may be asking yourself: why bother? They're just commas. What makes them so important?

There are two basic answers to those questions. First, if your reader *does* know the rules and you don't, sloppy comma usage could make you look bad—perhaps unprofessional or lazy about your writing. Second, having your commas in the right places can affect the meaning of your sentences, and they give the reader clear signals, showing how your ideas are connected. Remember that your main goal is effective communication of your ideas, getting them from your head into a reader's head. Everything we've looked at so far has an impact on this, and the lowly comma does, too.

Here are the rules to follow:

1. **Use commas to separate months from years and cities from states.**
    - He died on January 15, 1984 in Little Rock, Arkansas.

    Don't use a comma if the date is for the month and year only.
    - He died in January 1984.

2. **Use a comma before a coordinating conjunction when joining two independent clauses** (see the section on sentence boundaries above

for further explanation). The coordinating conjunctions are *for, and, nor, but, or, yet, so*.

- We were all hungry, but we had to wait an hour before getting seated.
- The airplane was overbooked, so I had to catch the next flight.
- Jack complained to the manager, and she gave him his money back.

Don't use a comma with a coordinating conjunction that is *not* joining independent clauses.

- Tracy *and* Jack waited for the bus.
- We walked for an hour *and* never saw another person.
- Either Gina *or* Sara will pick up the package.
- It was an old *but* valuable book that she lost.

3. **Use a comma to join a subordinating clause to an independent clause when the subordinating clause starts the sentence.**
   - After the show was over, we waited for a taxi.
   - Because she broke her leg, she couldn't finish her skiing class.
   - If someone asks you to take a package on board, you shouldn't do it.

   Don't use a comma if the order is reversed and the independent clause comes first.
   - She couldn't finish her skiing class because she broke her leg.

4. **Use a comma for introductory elements in a sentence.** These include infinitive phrases (*to* + the simple form of a verb), prepositional phrases longer than four words, and –ing phrases.
   - Thinking of the work I had to do, I decided not to stay.
   - To keep her daughter happy, she decided to buy the tickets.
   - For a whole month last year, we were lucky enough to live in Spain.

5. **Use a comma for introductory words.**
   - No, I haven't seen him this week.
   - Therefore, no harm was done.
   - However, she still wanted to find her cat.

- Well, I need to keep an open mind.

6. **Use a comma to connect closing words or phrases at the ends of sentences.** These include short questions.
    - Zelda told me she had voted for the winner, too.
    - You're going to meet there, aren't you?

7. **Use commas to separate three or more items or clauses in a series.**
    - I put a sandwich, an apple, and some pretzels in her lunch.
    - She attributes her success to hard work, dedication, and courage.
    - I read two magazines, I listened to three compact discs, and I still had time to kill before my flight.

Your Turn

Read the following paragraph and insert commas where necessary.

John Wilkes Booth shot President Abraham Lincoln on April 12 1865. The assassination occurred just days after the Civil War had ended and Booth felt that Lincoln was a tyrant and that he deserved to die for what had been done to the South. With several murderous accomplices, Booth planned to kill the President the Vice President and the Secretary of State. However only Booth succeeded in killing his victim. Hiding in the theater where Lincoln was watching a play Booth crept up behind the President and shot him in the back of the head before jumping down onto the stage and running out into the alley. Mortally wounded Lincoln was taken to a nearby house and he survived for nine hours before succumbing. A nationwide manhunt followed and Booth was eventually surrounded by soldiers and killed by one of them as the barn he was hiding in burned.

8. **Use a comma to separate non-essential elements from the rest of the sentence.** A non-essential phrase or clause is one not necessary to a reader's understanding of the sentence or to a portion of it that is being modified. Usually, this information will follow a noun, modifying it and often interrupting the flow of the sentence. Compare these examples:

- The man who was driving the red Corvette parked next us.
- My fiancé, who was driving the red Corvette, parked next to us.

In the first example, the clause *who was driving the red Corvette* gives us information identifying the man. In the second example, the noun *fiancé* is more specific than *man*, and the fact that he was driving a red Corvette does nothing to add to readers' understanding of who he is. That is, one generally has only one fiancé at a time. So, we need the commas in the second example because the information they contain is non-essential. Here are a few more examples:

- September, the hottest month last year, left me feeling miserable.
- She started working at Sears, the biggest store in the mall, to earn money for her trip.
- My wife, who was pregnant, waited in the car.
- He bought his Plymouth Roadrunner, a classic muscle car, before realizing how much it would cost to drive it.

Notice that the nouns being modified by the phrases or clauses are all very specific—proper names of a month, a store, and a car, or another very specific term like *wife*. Often, use of a proper name or a very specific term before the interrupting phrase or clause can be a clue as to whether or not the interrupting information is essential or not. Sometimes, though, it's not always so clear, and we have to rely on **context** to decide whether something is essential or not. Consider this example:

> The doctor who operated on me last month was just arrested for insurance fraud.

In this sentence, the clause *who operated on me last month* is essential to a reader's understanding of who the doctor is. The doctor has not been named, but the clause that follows it works to separate this doctor from all other doctors. Imagine reading this instead:

> The doctor was just arrested for insurance fraud.

Our response to this would probably be *Which doctor are you talking about?* Because we need the information in the *who* clause to help the sentence make sense, that information is **essential** and thus does not get set aside by commas. However, if the original sentence was put into context with another, the outcome might be different:

> I felt so fortunate to be introduced to the world-renowned specialist and for him to take an interest in my case, but now I wonder if it was such a good thing. The doctor, who operated on me last month, was just arrested for insurance fraud.

In this example, we still don't know the doctor's name, but now we know more about him. The first sentence identifies him as a *world-renowned specialist.* Since there are no other doctors being described in these sentences, it is only logical for readers to assume that the doctor in the second sentence is the same one mentioned in the first. In this case, the sentence would make just as much sense without *who operated on me last month.* Now the information is **non-essential** to our understanding of who the doctor is, so we set it apart with commas.

Your Turn

Read the following sentences, and place commas around non-essential elements.

In 1924, a few people had the unique experience of watching a remarkable film that would never be seen the same way again. The man who was responsible for the film was Erich von Stroheim a director who had made such films as *Foolish Wives* and *The Devil's Passkey* and was also well known for his acting roles playing villains so well that he had become known as "The Man You Love to Hate." When he began directing *Greed* which was based on Frank Norris' novel *McTeague* von Stroheim decided to shoot the book exactly as it was written rather than select key scenes from the novel to tell the basic story. The resulting film was more than eight hours long which was longer than any other film had ever been. People who saw test screenings reported that the film was like nothing they had experienced before. However, studio heads who feared that the film would fail because of its extreme length took control of the movie away from von

Stroheim. They cut the film down to just over two hours long which was thought to be a more marketable length and the remaining six hours were destroyed. While there have long been rumors that copies of the original version still exist in private vaults, none have ever surfaced.

9. **Use a comma to separate coordinate adjectives modifying the same term.** Coordinate adjectives carry the same weight; in other words, they modify the term equally, as opposed to **hierarchical** adjectives, which build on one another. If your adjectives are coordinate, one of them could be removed, or their order could be changed, and the meaning would still be clear. Another test is to see if the word *and* could be inserted between the adjectives. Here is an example:

    It was a bright, beautiful day with graceful, puffy clouds in a breathtaking blue sky.

    The first two adjectives—*bright* and *beautiful*—modify the word *day*. The second pair—*graceful* and *puffy*—modify *clouds*. The third pair—*breathtaking* and *blue*—modify *sky*. In the first two cases, the adjectives could be reversed, and the sentence would still make sense:

    It was a beautiful, bright day with puffy, graceful clouds in a breathtaking blue sky.

    However, the same could not be said of the final pair of modifiers—*breathtaking* and *blue*. If those words were reversed, the sentence would not sound right:

    It was a bright, beautiful day with graceful, puffy clouds in a blue breathtaking sky.

    Using the *and* test mentioned above, we can see that *and* could be inserted between the first two pairs of adjectives (*It was a bright and beautiful day*), but *and* would not make sense with the final pair. In other words, we would not say *blue and breathtaking sky*, so that tells us that those two adjectives are not coordinate, and a comma does not go between them.

    Here are a few more examples:

    - The bright, ripe apples looked ready for picking.
    - The worn out, old car had four flat tires.
    - We watched in horror as the fierce, swift tornado got closer.

But not:

- My mom likes to watch sad old movies. (we would not say *sad and old movies*)
- She sat and sipped her steaming hot coffee. (we would not say *steaming and hot coffee*)

Your Turn

The following sentences contain several adjectives. Decide which ones are coordinate adjectives and place commas accordingly.

When I opened the heavy wooden door, the smell of musty old books greeted me before my eyes could adjust to the dim muted light inside. The bookstore owner sat on a tall wobbly stool behind the counter, its cluttered glass top littered with books, newspapers and magazines. The friendly well-dressed old man nodded toward me and asked if he could help me find anything, but I told him I was just looking and then started pondering the packed sagging shelves. With a simple satisfied grin, I wandered from shelf to shelf, wondering if I would find a rare hidden treasure among the disarray. An hour later, I left having come up with nothing more than a cheap paperback copy of a book I'd been wanting to read for a long time. Even so, the act of hunting through the confusing crowded shelves and tall teetering piles of books placed here and there around the disorganized little store had been quite satisfying.

10. **Use commas to introduce quotation marks.** The following section explains quotation marks, including the use of commas and the other punctuation necessary to their proper use. It is best to read the comma rules for quotations along with the rest of the quotation rules.

Quotation Marks

Depending on the type of essay you are expected to write, you may or may not have the opportunity to use quotation marks right now, but the time will come. Quotations usually show up in narrative essays or documented research papers; however, it is possible for you to use them in expository or argumentative writing as well. Make sure you look up how and when to use quotations properly in the sections on Essays That Respond to a Text and Essays That Use Outside Sources. Here, we'll focus on proper punctuation for quotations.

1. When introducing a quotation, use a comma before the opening quotation mark and capitalize the first word in the quotation.
   - She shouted, "Look out!"
   - We listened as he said, "It's important that you pay attention."

   However, if you are quoting only a portion of what was said, do not use a comma to introduce the material, and do not capitalize the first word of the quoted material.
   - The minister said it was "good common sense" as well as faith that would serve us best.
   - The missing hiker said he had been saved by "dumb luck" and nothing more.

2. If the end of the quotation is also the end of the sentence, put the final period before the closing quotation mark.
   - I said, "Turn right at the light."
   - The doctor said, "I have some good news for you."

3. If the sentence continues past the end of the quotation, use a comma before the closing quotation mark and a period at the end of the sentence.
   - "I never pay attention to people like you," he sneered.
   - The captain said, "Wait here," and went in without us.
   - According to the lead researcher, "The main cause of the disease has not yet been discovered" (Smith 18).

4. If the quotation is interrupted, use a comma before the first closing quotation mark and another before the second opening quotation mark. Don't capitalize the first word in the second part of the quotation.
   - "I know we should go," she said, "but I think I'll stay."
   - "If you eat it before it's ripe," I said, "you'll be sorry."

   However, if the two parts of the quotation are actually separate sentences, then end the first sentence with a period before resuming the quotation, and use a capital letter after the second part of the quotation begins.

- "They've been gone three weeks," she said. "I don't think they'll be back."
- "It's in the basement," Joe said. "The cat must have dragged it in last night."

5. If the quoted material is a question, use a question mark before the closing quotation mark and no other punctuation after it.

   - With a raised eyebrow, she said, "And what do you mean by that?"
   - Relieved, he hugged the dog and said, "Where have you been?"

   However, if the sentence itself is a question and ends with a quotation that is *not* a question, place the question mark after the closing quotation mark with no other punctuation inside the quotation marks.

   - Do you agree with the saying, "A fool and his money are soon parted"?
   - Where can we find Hamlet saying, "The play's the thing"?

6. If you are using a quotation within a quotation, use single quotation marks to indicate the secondary quotation. If the secondary quotation comes at the end of the whole quotation, don't separate the single and double quotations with any punctuation.

   - The mayor said, "Let us not forget that we are 'a nation dedicated to the proposition that all men are created equal,' as Abraham Lincoln so poignantly reminded us."
   - Nervously, he told the policeman, "The mugger just looked at me and said, 'Shut up and give me your wallet.'"

7. Finally, it is also possible to use quotation marks to indicate sarcasm or to let the reader know that something is not necessarily what it seems. Rather than write the word *supposedly*, you can just put quotation marks around the word or phrase in question. For example:

   - The advertisement had said the trip was free. But by the time we finished paying all the hidden fees, our "free" trip cost us a thousand dollars.
   - Gina was shocked to find out what was really in her "organic" cereal.

Since this may be considered a bit informal, you should do this only sparingly.

Remember, too, that if you are writing out a conversation with quotations from more than one person, you need to start a new paragraph each time you quote a new speaker. It's also important to establish who is speaking, but once that's done, you don't have to write *he said* or *she said* with every quotation as long as it's clear for the reader exactly who is speaking.

> Yesterday, I ran into one of my Chemistry classmates whom I hadn't seen for several days. "Where have you been?" I asked.
>
> "They changed my work schedule," he answered.
>
> "Are you dropping Chemistry?"
>
> "No," he responded with a smile. "I didn't miss any other classes all semester, so the professor's going to let me come back next week once work gets back to normal."
>
> "Great! I'll see you then."

Your Turn

The following sentences include quotation marks but no other punctuation. Insert the correct punctuation.

1. "Welcome home" my mother said "We've missed you so much"
2. "If you want it fixed right" the mechanic said "it's going to cost twice as much as what I originally estimated"
3. He looked me in the eye and said "I can't stand it anymore"
4. Nervously, Jack said "Will you call me when you get there"
5. "I know I'm right. He definitely said 'turn left at the oak tree' but you wrote it down wrong" she said with frustration
6. How would you feel if someone said "Your money or your life"
7. "So Jefferson was right" the professor said "It all comes down to 'life, liberty, and the pursuit of happiness'"

Apostrophes

There are two reasons for using apostrophes—to make contractions and to show possession.

Contractions should be avoided in most academic writing, but occasionally there are places where they are appropriate, especially in narrative essays where the author's tone is usually more relaxed than in expository or argumentative essays. Errors with contractions usually occur when students forget to use the apostrophes, but there are a few problems that can occur when words get confused.

It's and *Its.* Remember that *It's* with an apostrophe means *it is* or *it has.* There are no exceptions. *Its* without the apostrophe indicates possession. If you write, "The cat chased it's tail," the sentence is actually saying, "The cat chased it is tail." Not only is this not what you meant, but it doesn't make any sense, and a reader who knows the rules will be able to see that.

You're and *Your.* Remember that *You're* with an apostrophe is a contraction for *you are* and that *Your* indicates possession. If you write, "You should know you're rights," the sentence actually means, "You should know you are rights." Like the example above, this doesn't make any sense. The correct sentence would be "You should know your rights."

Should've, *Would've,* and *Could've* are contractions for *should have, would have* and *could have.* As contractions, these are far too informal to be used in academic writing and should be avoided. Even worse mistakes occur, however, because students often assume that the phrase is *should of* or *could of* because those phrases sound like *should've* and *could've.* Remember that while using *should've* is too informal, using *should of* is simply wrong and reveals far more about a writer's shortcomings. Don't make this mistake.

Possessives are words, usually ending in apostrophe-s, that show ownership or some characteristic trait. As with contractions, there are usually no problems. However, there are some words that can get confusing when they are written as possessives. Here are the basic rules for showing possession.

1. To make most nouns possessive, simply add an apostrophe-s:
    - The cat moved her tail. →The cat's tail moved.
    - The plane had icy wings. →The plane's wings were icy.

2. If a single-syllable noun ends in -s, add an apostrophe-s
    - He dated the boss's daughter.
    - The bus's engine would not start.

3. If a multiple-syllable noun ends in -s, add an apostrophe without an -s.
    - Mr. Harris' car is parked across the street.

4. If a noun adds an -s to form a plural, add an apostrophe without another -s to make it possessive.
    - We examined each one of the applicants' resumes.
    - I borrowed my parents' car on Saturday.

5. If a noun does not add an -s to form a plural, add an apostrophe-s to make it possessive.
    - The children's shoes were wet after they splashed in the puddles.
    - The researcher made sure to get the women's opinions.

Another problem with apostrophes occurs with words that change their endings to form plurals, and students sometimes get confused about whether they should use the plural or possessive form of the word.

Don't write:

I paid attention to my families needs.
(This sounds like the writer has more than one family, and there is no apostrophe to indicate possession.)

Instead, write:

I paid attention to my family's needs.
(Now the writer has one family, and the apostrophe is there to indicate that the needs are those of the family.)

Don't write:

Every morning, we pledge allegiance to our countries flag.
(This sounds like there is more than one country, and there is no apostrophe to indicate possession.)

Instead, write:

Every morning, we pledge allegiance to our country's flag. *(Now it is clear that there is one country whose flag is being given allegiance.)*

Your Turn

There are several errors with apostrophes in the following paragraph, including missing apostrophes, apostrophes where they don't belong, and confusion between contractions and possessives. Correct the errors as you find them.

My car wouldn't start on Tuesday morning, so I had to borrow my parent's car to get to school. Its a bit embarrassing driving their car because my moms really into recycling and bags filled with bottle's and can's are in the backseat, ready to go to the recycling center. I dont mind that she recycle's, of course. It's been one of my families tradition's for as long as I can remember. Its just that it's kind of hard when you're car looks like a rolling trashcan with all those bags in the back. When I got to school, I parked as far away from the building's as I could, but I would of parked farther away if it had been possible. I decided it would be better to ride my bike if I couldnt get my own car fixed right away.

Acknowledgements

This book could not have been written without help, support, and encouragement from many people.

I am especially grateful to the Board of Trustees of the North Orange County Community College District for granting me a sabbatical leave to conduct research on the book. Special thanks also go to the members of the NOCCCD sabbatical committee who recommended my application for approval, and to Fullerton College President Kathleen Hodge for reading and endorsing the application. I was fortunate enough to receive support in the form of letters of recommendation from Humanities Division Dean Dan Willoughby, English Department Coordinator Jeanne Costello, and my colleague and friend, Tamara Trujillo. The sabbatical application would not have been nearly as successful without generous assistance and advice from Bruce Henderson.

During the drafting phase of the book, several of my colleagues agreed to field test an early version in their classes, and I am grateful to them for volunteering to help me this way and for providing insightful feedback. They were: Nadine Arndt, Liz Kiszely, Annie Liu, Kim Orlijan, and Tamara Trujillo. Students in each of their classes also completed surveys about the book, which provided extremely valuable feedback.

Special thanks go to Donna Barnard at Orange Coast College for encouragement and support in the early phases of my research.

I have also received feedback and support from Mark Knoernschild and loads of encouragement from everyone else in the English Department at Fullerton College. Jeanne Costello's ideas about essay development were especially helpful. I feel truly fortunate to be surrounded by such supportive colleagues.

This book has grown out of many years of teaching, and so I must also thank the countless students with whom I've worked over the last twenty years. They didn't know it at the time, but they were essentially teaching me how to teach, and much of the advice in this book has grown out of my experiences with them. Special acknowledgement goes to the students who allowed me to reproduce their work in these pages: Scott Brandes, Shannon Goldsmith, and Mike Pita Vega.

This most recent version of the book was also made possible through assistance and encouragement from Casey Kelly and Peggy Henderson at McGraw-Hill. Many thanks.

Finally, I must thank my wife, Kari, and daughter, Olive, for giving me the time needed to work on this project and for encouraging me every step of the way. Who could ask for anything more?